Date Due

Atlas of the World
in the
MIDDLE AGES

Above: 11th-century statues of Buddha at Polonnawura, Sri Lanka. Right: A page from a copy of the Gospels known as the Book of Kells. It was made by Celtic monks in about AD 800. The Celts, who had once spread from the Rhine to the British Isles, now lived on the western edge of Europe, in Scotland, Ireland, Wales, Cornwall and Brittany. Below: Muslim soldiers, known as Saracens, go into battle during the Crusades. Below right: An enamelled pendant made by the Byzantines in about 1000. Previous page: A 14th-century bust of Charlemagne made to hold parts of his skull.

Editorial

Consultant
Lionel Butler

Adviser
Brian Adams

Authors
Brian Adams
Christopher Fagg
Frances Halton
Robert Knox
Keith Lye

Editor
Frances M. Clapham

Published 1981 by Warwick Press,
730 Fifth Avenue, New York, New York, 10019

First published in Great Britain by Longman Group Limited in 1980.

Copyright © 1980 by Grisewood & Dempsey Ltd.

Printed by Vallardi Industrie Grafiche, Milan, Italy.

6 5 4 3 2 1

SBN 0-531-09179-1

Library of Congress Catalog Card No. 80-52129

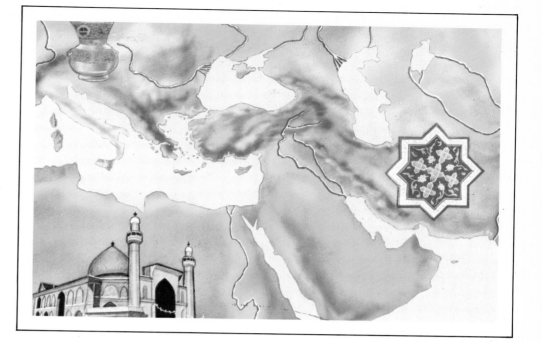

Contents

Top centre: A detail of a picture from a 15th-century 'Book of Hours'. Above: Part of the Islamic world. Left: An ornate brooch made by 'barbarian' craftsmen. Below: Citizens of Florence burn luxurious vanities as commanded by Savonarola.

After the Romans

During the Middle Ages many pilgrims made long journeys, often on foot, to visit places connected with saints. This pilgrim badge, showing St Michael, is in Salisbury museum in south-west England.

The religion of Islam, which began in Arabia in the 7th century, soon spread all through the Near East. This picture, painted in Baghdad in 1237, shows the market scene.

The Middle Ages is a term historians use to describe the period in Europe between the fall of the Western Roman empire and the beginning of the modern age of science, exploration, and widespread knowledge. In the rest of the world, too, this was a time of growth and change, which were to some extent connected with what happened in Europe. All settled areas of civilization found themselves threatened by barbaric peoples during this period. By AD 500 the Roman empire in western Europe had fallen to Germanic peoples from across the Rhine. India and China had been attacked by the nomadic Huns of Central Asia, some of whom had also threatened Europe.

The Break-up of the Western Empire

At its greatest the Roman empire was well administered, strongly defended and prosperous. It united millions of people, from Britain to the Near East, in a way of life based on cities, trade, organized agriculture and a code of laws written in a single language–Latin. From the 4th century Christianity provided another strong link. From the 3rd century, however, this great unified empire began to decay from within. The western provinces, Gaul, Spain, Britain and Italy, suffered a decline in trade and population. Administering the west, and defending the long Rhine-Danube frontier, became increasingly difficult.

At the same time, the empire faced increasing threats from outside. In the wild forests and marshlands to the east lived warlike Germanic peoples. Their way of life was based on farming but included constant raiding and warfare: for them, the highest virtues were courage and loyalty in battle. To the Romans they were 'barbarians'. From the end of the 3rd century these peoples stepped up their raids across the Rhine and the Danube.

Fall of the Empire

The period from the 3rd to the 8th century is often called the Age of Migrations. It was a time of tremendous upheaval as the peoples of eastern and central Europe moved westwards towards the frontiers of the Roman empire. The Romans were forced to admit some of these peoples into the empire. They gave them lands and privileges in return for which the barbarians became *foederati* (allies) charged with defending the borders. Shortly after 400, there were new upheavals. The Huns, savage nomads from Central Asia, drove westwards across Europe. Germanic Goths, Vandals, Burgundians and, later, Franks crossed into Gaul, pushing deeply into the western provinces. The Romanized populations were forced to give them the lands they needed. The Germanic peoples set up kingdoms in Gaul, Spain, North Africa and Italy where a Gothic chieftain, Odoacer, deposed the last western Roman emperor, Romulus Augustulus, in AD 476. The eastern Roman empire survived to become the Byzantine empire (see page 14).

The 'Dark Ages'

Over the next century the barbarian kings struggled to hold on to and expand their territories. This time was once thought of as a Dark Age, when civilization perished. But, however much they had run down, Roman law and administration were too well established to disappear overnight. Rulers still hoped to rebuild a great European empire on Roman lines–even if their ideas of the old empire were rather hazy and inaccurate. The Christian Church had not been destroyed and in the next few centuries many more people were converted to Christianity. Churchmen travelled from one country to another. Many monasteries were built. Their monks spent much time studying and they sent missionaries to pagan lands. Christians had a common belief, a spiritual leader in the pope, and a common cause for which they would unite and fight when necessary. In 1054, however, the Christian Church split. The Christians of Asia Minor refused to accept the authority of the pope and formed the Eastern Orthodox Church centred on Constantinople. The Eastern Church spread to many people in eastern Europe.

Nevertheless, Europe was in a bad state. Undoubtedly people continued to work the land and gather the harvest. But old patterns

The Vikings threatened Europe between 800 and 1100. In the 13th and 14th centuries, Mongol hordes under Genghis Khan and Timur the Lame scoured Asia from east to west. But by 1500 a more settled picture had emerged. Europe was beginning to develop into a patchwork of powerful nation-states. Rulers of the Islamic faith controlled North Africa, the eastern Mediterranean countries and Asia as far as India. In China, the Ming Dynasty controlled a splendid empire. Trade routes by land and sea linked Europe and the Far East. As the number of contacts increased, Europeans began to look for new trade routes. The Age of Exploration was about to dawn which would finally link all the places in the world where settled civilizations existed.

Below: The Catalan map, made in the late 14th century for the king of France. The increase in trade led to the need for, and making of, increasingly accurate maps.

The many great stone cathedrals and churches built in Europe in the Middle Ages remind us of the strength of Christianity at that time. Notre Dame cathedral, Paris (above) was begun in 1163 and was a model for many later French churches.

Below: A gold coin showing Theodoric (454–526), who founded the Ostrogothic kingdom in Italy. Theodoric had spent nine years in Constantinople, and the Byzantine emperor supported him in Italy. The Roman senate also gave him their full support.

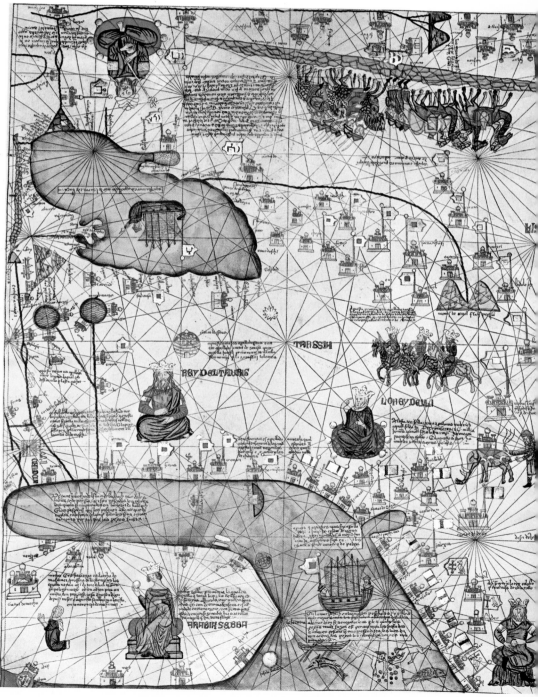

of trade had been changed and travel was difficult and dangerous. Kings had to hand over local government to their sons and relatives. In return for grants of land barbarian nobles and leading churchmen protected their territory, administered local affairs, and received most of the produce. In this system can be seen the roots of later feudalism, the way of life which dominated Europe during much of the Middle Ages.

The World in AD 500

Migrating barbarians over the last few centuries have overthrown the Gupta empire in India and invaded north China. In western Europe they have settled throughout the Western Roman empire; lacking a central organization, they develop a number of small states linked increasingly by their common Christianity. The stronger Eastern Roman (Byzantine) empire remains and Roman laws and learning are upheld there. In the 7th century the new religion of Islam spreads quickly through the Near East and North Africa.

3 Northern Europe Saxons, Angles, and Jutes settle in England; the Celts thrive in Wales, Cornwall, Scotland, Brittany in north-west France, and especially in Ireland. They are converted to Christianity. Scandinavia is dominated by pagan warrior farmers.

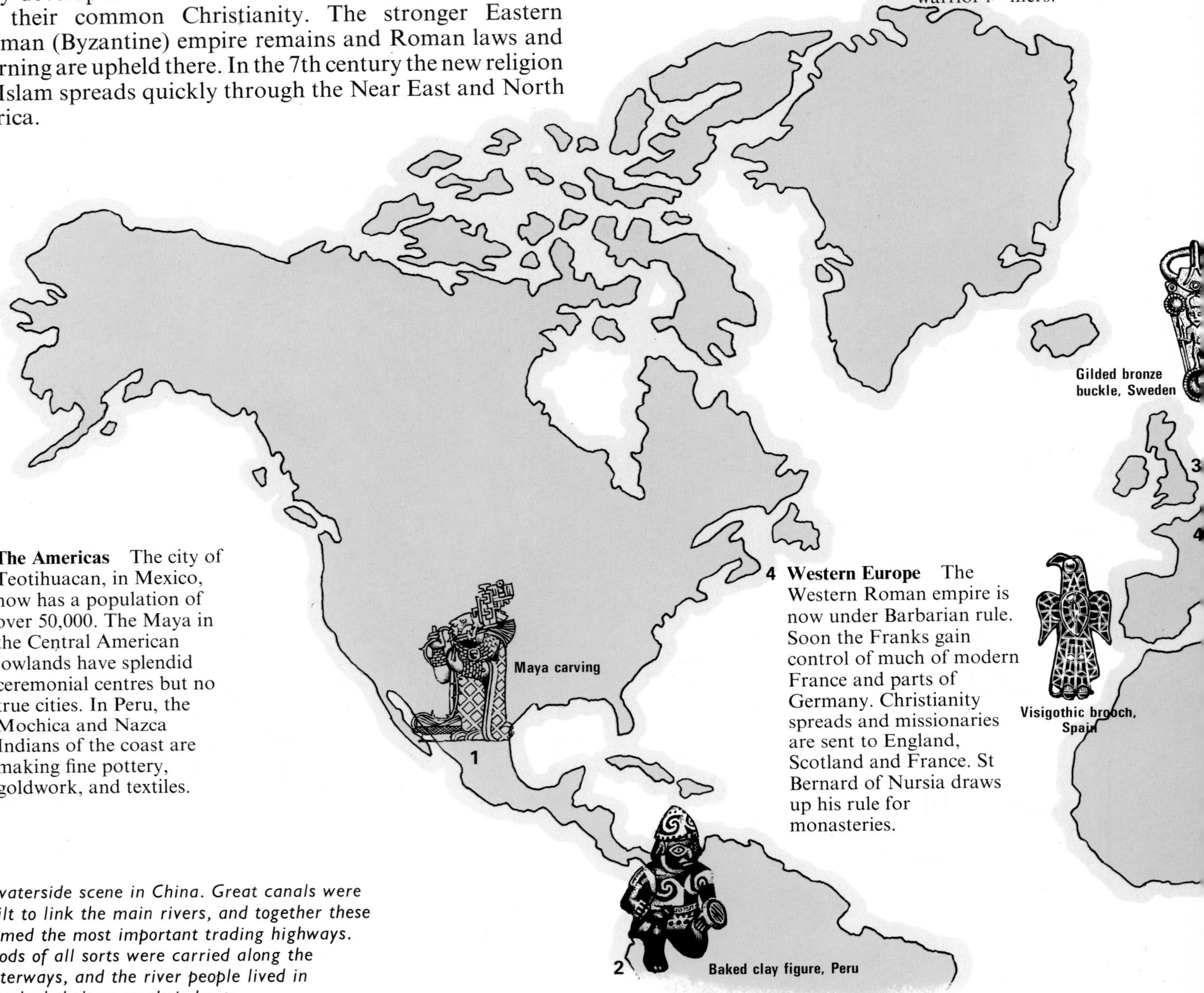

Gilded bronze buckle, Sweden

1 The Americas The city of Teotihuacan, in Mexico, now has a population of over 50,000. The Maya in the Central American lowlands have splendid ceremonial centres but no true cities. In Peru, the
2 Mochica and Nazca Indians of the coast are making fine pottery, goldwork, and textiles.

Maya carving

4 Western Europe The Western Roman empire is now under Barbarian rule. Soon the Franks gain control of much of modern France and parts of Germany. Christianity spreads and missionaries are sent to England, Scotland and France. St Bernard of Nursia draws up his rule for monasteries.

Visigothic brooch, Spain

Baked clay figure, Peru

A waterside scene in China. Great canals were built to link the main rivers, and together these formed the most important trading highways. Goods of all sorts were carried along the waterways, and the river people lived in thatched shelters on their boats.

The 'barbarians' who moved into Europe were farming people. They lived in simple wooden houses and cleared the forests for land. Their warriors were skilled fighters, and they had a long tradition of poetry.

Barbarian rider. a Frankish belt buckle

Pottery tomb figure, Japan

Gold brooch, Germany

Sassanian silver dish, Persia

Gilt bronze figure, China

Sculpture of Buddha, India

Brooches like this were used by the barbarians to pin their cloaks. They were very skilled jewellers and metalworkers.

5 **The Byzantine Empire** The Eastern Roman empire, from now on known as the Byzantine empire, remains strong enough to bribe or beat off the barbarians. In the mid-6th century Justinian reconquers much of the former Roman land in North Africa and Italy.

6 **Near East** In 571 the Prophet Muhammad is born in Mecca in Arabia; he founds the religion of Islam which spreads with astonishing speed through the Near East.

7 **China** The Tartar rulers of the north are adopting Chinese ways. In 618 China is reunited under the T'ang dynasty and a time of great prosperity and artistic activity begins.

Technology

During the Middle Ages many inventions and discoveries were made, and old ways of doing things were improved. Many new ideas came from the East, and were brought west by traders. The Muslims learnt a number of skills, including papermaking, from China and brought to Europe the 'Arabic' numbering system learned from the Hindus of India. They were also clever astronomers, chemists, and doctors. Technology in Europe suffered a setback with the barbarian invasions, when many of the Roman techniques were partly or even completely lost. However, the barbarians themselves were immensely skilled metalworkers. As Europe became more settled again, new developments were made which improved agriculture, transport and manufacture.

Farming

Farming was the most widespread way of life in the Middle Ages. In the East great irrigation schemes allowed new land to be cultivated, and in Europe forests were cleared and marshes drained for ploughland and pasture. As iron became common, tools were improved; spades and forks were shod with iron and new tools like the long-handled scythe were developed. A three-year crop rotation system was used in much of Europe instead of the Roman two-year system. Ploughs were improved by a mouldboard to turn over the soil (a device used by the Chinese some 2000 years earlier). Teams of oxen were used for ploughing, and in the late Middle Ages ploughhorses were also used.

This mosque lamp was made in Syria in the 13th century. The Muslims found an old-established glass industry here which they developed. Muslim glass was prized for its beauty.

Right: A page from a Bible printed by Johannes Gutenberg of Mainz, who in the 1450s invented printing with movable metal type. Before this, books had to be copied by hand. This was slow and expensive and mistakes were easily made. Gutenberg made a separate mould for each letter and the letters were then cast in metal. They could be used again and again. He arranged the letters into words, and then clamped them together on a crude wine press. He inked them with a new kind of oil-based ink, and then pressed a sheet of paper against them. He could print up to 300 sheets a day.

The invention of the padded horsecollar was a great advance, as it allowed horses to pull heavy weights. This picture of farming in October comes from a 15th-century book called 'Les Très Riches Heures du duc de Berry', and is one of a series showing work on the land in the different months.

Watermills became more common. The Domesday Book tells us that in 1086 there were 5624 in England south of the Trent. They were used for milling corn and later for industries; fulling mills were an important part of cloth-processing, and water-power operated hammers and bellows for the metal industry. Windmills were used in Iran in the 7th century. They were used first to pump water and later to grind corn. Windmills became common in Europe in the 13th century.

Travel and transport

At the end of the 9th century three inventions spread rapidly through Europe which had a great effect on travel and transport. One was the stirrup. A little toe stirrup was used in India in about AD 100, but stirrups were not used in China until the 5th century. Stirrups not only made riding more comfortable but also made mounted knights more efficient. Now they could stand in the saddle and use their swords over a much wider range, and they were less easily unhorsed by their enemies. Towards the end of the 9th century nailed horseshoes were used in Europe, which meant that horses could travel longer distances and carry heavier burdens. A little later the rigid, padded horsecollar came into use. Before this, the horse had been harnessed with a breastband. When a horse pulled hard this pressed against its windpipe, and choked it. The horsecollar meant that horses could pull much heavier weights, and now waggoners and carters could transport much greater loads over longer distances.

GUNPOWDER

One of the most important inventions of the Middle Ages was that of gunpowder and cannon. Some time in the 10th century the Chinese discovered that crushed nitre, sulphur and charcoal mixed in the right proportions would explode. From there the invention spread to the west.

The use of guns meant the end of medieval warfare. Cannonballs could smash through metal armour, and could break down castle walls. The medieval era of armed knights, based in stone-walled castles, was over.

In about 1321 the first cannon were used in Europe. They were made by Italians and fired by Chinese gunpowder. This picture shows the siege of La Rochelle in France at the end of the 14th century. In the foreground is a primitive cannon. It is made of iron rods welded and bound together.

BUILDING

The most common material for important buildings in medieval Europe was stone. An architect would draw up plans or sometimes make a model. Over a thousand men would work under him on a cathedral. Stone was cut at the quarry by roughmasons, who also laid and mortared the blocks in place. The important carving was done by freemasons. Wooden scaffolding was used for the building, with cranes operated by donkeys or even men to lift the stones. Masons' tools were much the same as those used today: saws, chisels, wedges, and mallets. Many other craftsmen, including carpenters, glaziers, painters, and metalworkers, all helped to make the great cathedrals that were one of the chief glories of the Middle Ages.

Shipping

Advances in ship building helped traders and fishermen in the Middle Ages and made possible the later explorations. Two such inventions came from the East. One was the lateen (triangular) sail, which made it possible for ships to beat into the wind. It was used from the 9th century on in the Mediterranean. Four centuries later hinged stern-post rudders came into use in the eastern Mediterranean; they made ships much easier to steer. At this time, too, magnetic compasses were becoming common and good charts began to be made.

Cloth-making was one of the most important industries of the Middle Ages, and several inventions helped cloth production. They included the spinning wheel, the horizontal frame loom, and the fulling mill, in which cloth was thickened by being beaten with water-driven mallets. The cloth trade brought great wealth to cities, including those of Flanders and northern Italy. This carving of a weaver, by the 13th-century sculptor Pisano, is in Florence museum.

Metalworking

The barbarian invaders of Europe were skilled metalworkers, producing fine jewellery and weapons. All through the Middle Ages magnificent metal objects were made. Many of them were very elaborate. Bronze was easily cast in moulds. Gold and silver were sometimes cast but more often cut from a thin sheet and hammered into shape. A mixture of gold powder and mercury was used for gilding other metals. This liquid was painted on and the object heated until the mercury evaporated and the gold melted into a thin film.

Metal armour was vital to the knights of the Middle Ages. At first they used mail, made of iron wire rings welded together. Later they had plate armour. In Europe the iron had to be forged into shape with continuous heating and hammering, until the end of the Middle Ages. Then furnaces were developed which could reach high enough temperatures to melt the iron so that it could be cast into shape. In China, however, cast iron had been produced since the 5th century BC!

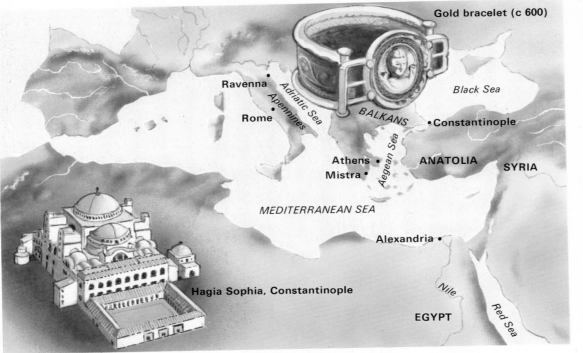

Gold bracelet (c 600)

CHRONOLOGY

527	Justinian emperor of Eastern (Byzantine) empire to 565. His forces conquer North Africa, Italy and South-eastern Spain
568	Lombards invade Italy and take north and centre
602	War with Persia; Slavs invade Balkans (to 628)
634	Arabs conquer Syria, Palestine and Egypt (to 642)
717	Arabs besiege Constantinople (to 718)
751	Ravenna falls to Lombards
826	Crete and Sicily fall to Arabs
863	Defeat of Arabs; Byzantines begin offensive in East
960	Empire expands and strengthens under Basil II (to 1025)
1071	Byzantine army defeated by Seljuk Turks
1204	Capture of Constantinople by Crusaders
1453	Constantinople falls to Turks

The Byzantine Empire

The huge empire built by the Romans did not completely disappear with the fall of Rome and the conquest of western Europe by the 'barbarians'. The eastern part, including the Balkans, Greece, Turkey, Syria, Palestine and Egypt, was richer and stronger than the west. It was able to drive off, or buy off, the invaders. It was ruled from Byzantium and for that reason it is known as the Byzantine empire. Byzantium was a small Greek port converted by the Roman emperor Constantine in AD 330 into a great capital for the Eastern Roman empire. He called it Constantinople, and Istanbul, its modern name, is the Turkish form of Constantinople.

The emperor had chosen the site for his city very carefully. It is on a promontary or triangle of land and commands the sea route between the Black Sea and the Mediterranean. Trade routes from the mainland of Europe led through Constantinople to the Near East and on to China. Ships from the Mediterranean sea could bring their goods into the safety of the city's excellent natural harbour.

The Romans gave the Byzantine empire its laws and its ways of government. But before Roman times the whole area had come under the Greek rule of Alexander the Great and his successors. Many rich cities on the coast of Anatolia had been founded by Greek colonists centuries earlier. The common language of the area was still Greek. In Constantinople, Ephesus Alexandria in Egypt and other centres the learning of the ancient Greeks was kept alive by learned men and women. Side by side with them were the new Christian scholars, for from its beginning Constantinople was a Christian city.

Running the Empire

The emperor's court was run with traditions and ceremonies which never varied. A large number of officials controlled the towns and the trade which passed through them. There was an elaborate customs service. Farther afield, Byzantine power was maintained by well-trained diplomats, who skilfully set the many enemies of the empire against one another.

The Byzantines made a great deal of beautiful jewellery. This gold and enamel pendant, showing St George, dates from about 1000.

Below: The walls of Constantinople were built in the 4th and 5th centuries to defend the city against the barbarians. They were never stormed until 1203.

Life in the Country

Under Byzantine rule huge areas of land were in the hands of wealthy, often quarrelsome, landowners. In the villages, peasants kept small herds of sheep or cattle. The land they worked varied from the rich fields of Egypt to the dry scrubland of central Anatolia (later Turkey). A drought or plagues of locusts sometimes ruined large areas. Taxes were heavy and it was hard for poor people to save money. They were tied to their land. The only way for them to get a better life was by running away to the towns or, if they were young men, by joining the army. Yet it was possible for a humble man to do well. The emperor Justinian came from a peasant family.

The Shrinking Empire

Persians, Arabs, Avars, Slavs, and finally Turks all conquered large parts of the Byzantine empire. By 1453 only the area around Constantinople was left. On Monday 28th May that year, the Ottoman Turks led by Sultan Mehmet II captured the city (see page 57). The last Greek emperor, called Constantine like the founder of the city, died during the final attack. His body was never found.

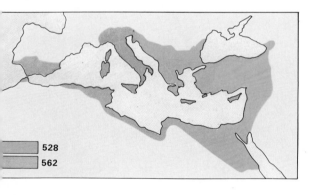

528
562

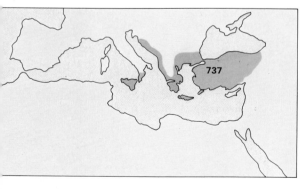

737

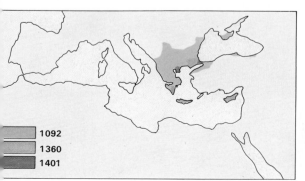

1092
1360
1401

TRADE

The Byzantine empire was rich in natural resources. Greece provided wine, olives, and olive oil which was used in cooking. Grain for export was produced in huge quantities along the coasts of North Africa, the Aegean and the eastern Mediterranean. (Some of these areas are now far more barren than they were in those days because the land has been worked too hard.) Glass and cotton came from Egypt and Syria. Syria also produced silk, which was in great demand for luxurious clothes and costly coverings for furniture. Large quantities of gold came from Anatolia, while papyrus, used to write on, came from Egypt as it had in the time of the Pharaohs. Other trade goods included timber and building stone, fish, meat and leather, salt, and dried fruits.

The goods produced inside the empire were traded for luxuries from far afield. China was the main source of silk. From India and the Far East came spices, sapphires and pearls. Africa provided ivory and gold, from Senegal and Ghana and possibly from as far south as Zimbabwe (Rhodesia). The north traded Russian furs and Baltic amber. Great trading or 'caravan' routes were established from Samarkand, the Indian Ocean and the Caspian Sea. To the west, Byzantine goods reached as far as Britain.

These maps show how the Byzantine empire shrank from its greatest under Justinian to a tiny remnant shortly before it was finally conquered by the Turks.

The Byzantine empire was at its greatest under the emperor Justinian (527–565). His general Belisarius conquered Sicily, Italy and parts of North Africa. This portrait of Justinian comes from the church of San Vitale in Ravenna, which was the capital of the Byzantine empire in Italy. Justinian organized existing Roman laws into a system known as the Code of Justinian.

An ivory carving possibly of the Byzantine empress Irene (752–803). Born in Athens, she reigned as regent for her young son from 780 to 790, and ruled again from 797 to 802.

The Near East

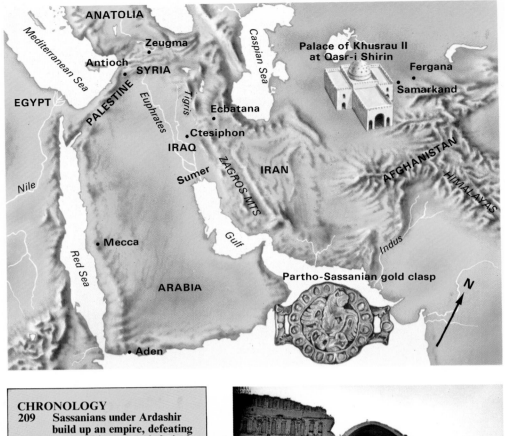

The Near East is a vast area, stretching from the Mediterranean in the west, eastwards through Iraq and Iran to the Indian subcontinent. To the north lies Russia, and to the south the Indian Ocean and the Gulf. A great deal of the area is mountainous, and it includes the great deserts of Syria and Arabia. There are also many valleys with good farmland, and the flood plains of the rivers Tigris and Euphrates in Iraq are so fertile that one of the first great civilizations of the ancient world grew up there round Sumer.

In the 4th century BC Alexander the Great of Macedon brought all the Near East under his rule. After he died, his lands were divided up between his generals. By the early centuries AD the lands along the Mediterranean were ruled by Rome, while those east of the Euphrates were controlled by an Iranian tribe, the Parthians.

In the 3rd century AD the Parthians were overthrown by another Iranian people, the Sassanians. They built up an empire which by the 7th century stretched from Afghanistan to the Mediterranean. Hardly had they conquered Egypt when the Muslims swept through the entire region, conquering it for the new faith of Islam.

CHRONOLOGY	
209	Sassanians under Ardashir build up an empire, defeating the Parthians overwhelmingly in 224
244	Shapur I defeats the Romans under Philip the Arab and later under Valerian
460	Hephthalite Huns control a large empire centred on Afghanistan (to 530)
531–579	Khusrau I re-establishes the Persian empire, gaining land from Byzantium, defeating Hephthalites, and making southern Arabia a dependency
571	Muhammad born in Mecca
612–620	Persians overrun Near East
622	Byzantines regain Anatolia and invade Mesopotamia (627). Khusrau II is murdered in a revolt
637	Muslim Arabs defeat Sassanians

Ruins of Khusrau I's palace at Ctesiphon, the most famous of all Sassanian buildings. The great arch is nearly 35 metres (115 feet) high and 50 metres (165 feet) long.

The Sassanians

The Sassanians came to power in the 3rd century AD. They soon came into conflict with the Romans to the west. They defeated them on a number of occasions, and great reliefs carved in the rocks tell the stories of their triumphs. Roman prisoners were settled all through the empire and used for cheap and often highly skilled labour. The ruins of the bridges they built can still be seen today. Conflict in the west continued in the time of the Byzantine empire there.

During the late 4th and 5th centuries the Near East, like other areas, was devastated by the invasions of the Huns. Some of them, known as Hephthalites, settled in Bactria in the north-east and built up an empire there. Here too the Sassanians had to fight frequent wars.

The peninsula of Arabia was the home of Bedouin tribes, who then as now lived in tents and moved around with their flocks in search of grazing. Arabia also had trading, manufacturing and fishing towns, and crops were grown in the big oases.

TRADE

Through the Near East ran the great overland trade routes which linked the western world with India and China. The Parthians made trading contacts with Rome on the one hand, and China on the other. Silks and precious stones, spices and scent flooded through the area, in return for Roman gold, and the Parthians grew rich as middlemen. Caravans started at Antioch in Syria and crossed the Euphrates at Zeugma. Then they went over the Zagros Mountains to Ecbatana and east to Samarkand, Fergana, and onwards to China. Other goods were carried by sea, sailing from India into the Gulf.

The sea routes for trade became important when the Huns were devastating Central Asia. The Sassanians extended their rule all along the north coast of the Indian Ocean, from the Gulf east to the delta of the Indus Valley. They prevented ships from other countries from buying direct from Indian merchants. When Arab traders tried to break the Sassanians' monopoly, Khusrau made southern Arabia a dependency, based ships in Aden and controlled the entrance to the Red Sea.

Part of a relief carving at Taq-i-Bustan. It shows Khusrau II standing in a boat and shooting at a great boar.

A 15th-century illustration to the story of Khusrau II and Queen Shirin, a favourite of Persia poets.

LUXURIOUS LIVING

The Sassanians loved luxury and good living. Cities like those at Bishapur and Ctesiphon had palaces decorated with sculptures, their walls painted or covered with glass mosaics. Floors too were decorated with mosaics or covered with silk carpets patterned like gardens. Vessels of gold and silver were skilfully decorated. The Sassanians loved jewellery, and Khusrau I wore clothes embroidered with gold thread. His enormous crown, made of gold and silver and decorated with precious stones, seems to have been so heavy that it had to be hung on a chain from the roof over the throne.

This Sassanian dish of gilded silver dates from the 7th or 8th century. Its decoration shows the mythical senmurw, part dog and part bird.

Khusrau

In 531 Khusrau I became ruler of the Sassanians. Their empire was impoverished by wars, famine and a heavy tribute paid each year to the Hephthalite Huns to the north-east. Khusrau made peace with the Byzantines to the west and kept up the tribute payments. He set about bringing prosperity to his country. The land was surveyed in such detail that every fruit and olive tree was counted. Then an annual tax was set, to be paid in money and not in kind. Great irrigation works were carried out to bring more land into use, and when villagers had no seed to sow the state provided it. Khusrau was also remembered for his justice.

Some of the tax money was spent in building up a strong army and strengthening the frontiers. In 540 Khusrau was ready to strike. He invaded Syria and captured Antioch, where he found large amounts of gold and silver. He joined forces with nomad Turks to defeat the Hephthalites, and added much of Afghanistan to his empire.

Khusrau's grandson, Khusrau II, extended the empire in the west. His armies overran the Near East, capturing Syria, Palestine and all Egypt. Meanwhile, however, a new threat was growing from an unexpected direction. The Arabs, converted to Islam (see page 21), were seeking to spread their Faith by conquering and converting the countries nearest to them. In an amazingly short time all the Near East was under their control. But they took up many of the good things in Sassanian life, to become part of the civilization of Islam.

The Franks

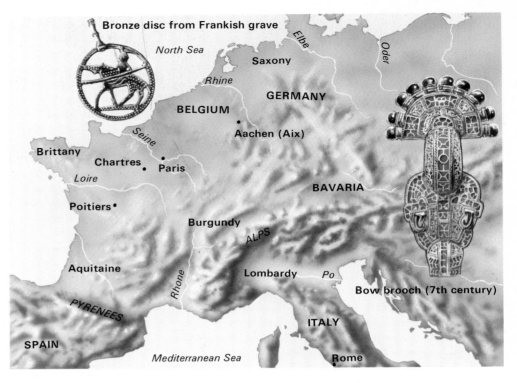

Bronze disc from Frankish grave

Bow brooch (7th century)

The kingdom of the West Franks was the greater part of modern France, a large country with a coastline which faces the Mediterranean in the south and the Atlantic in the north. High mountains separate the country from Spain and Italy, but the north is open to the Netherlands and Germany. Northern invaders can advance without much difficulty. In the Middle Ages, the north was rich in corn and dairy products, and olive oil and wine were the special produce of the south. Barley was a common crop, used to make porridge, beer and bread. Beans, peas and lentils were widely grown, providing the bulk of the peasant's diet, as meat was rarely eaten. Bees were kept for honey (the only sweetener) and this was sometimes used to make an alcoholic drink called mead, a kind of strong wine. Beer and wine were made according to the region. France has wide rivers and fish were plentiful. During the winter dried fish was an important food. The rivers were much used for transport and strings of barges were in use quite early on in the Frankish period.

The First Franks

Under the Romans, France had been known as Gaul. It was a settled and prosperous region. There were a number of large estates and thriving trading towns; many people had become Christian and bishoprics were set up. Towards the end of the Roman period, administration broke down (see page 8). Bands of robbers, often slaves in revolt, terrorized large areas. Tribes of 'barbarians' from east of the Rhine moved into Gaul and settled there.

Early in the 5th century a small tribe from western Germany crossed the Rhine into Gaul. They were called the Franks. By the end of the 5th century two Frankish kings, Childeric and his son Clovis, had gained control over much of modern France and West Germany. King Clovis became a Christian, which gained him the support of the many Christians in Gaul. He was also recognized as king by the Byzantine emperor Anastasius. When he died in 511, Clovis's sons succeeded him. They are known as the Merovings. They brought still more of western Europe under their control.

Charlemagne was revered as the defender of Christianity, and many legends grew up about him. Some are illustrated in this 13th-century window at Chartres. He was canonized as a saint in the 12th century.

Right: A gold coin of Charlemagne's time.

The Emperor Charlemagne

The greatest of all the Frankish kings was Charlemagne, whose father Pepin seized the throne from the Merovings. Charlemagne was a large, strong man, who was tough and brave. His name means 'Charles the Great'. He was fond of swimming and hunting, but he encouraged learning, and built himself a palace at Aachen (Aix) in Germany where Byzantine art and architecture were copied.

Charlemagne came to the throne in 768, and spent almost all of his reign at war. At first he fought against his Christian neighbours, bringing the people of Aquitaine, Brittany and Burgundy firmly under his control. At the pope's request, he subdued the Lombards of northern Italy and was crowned their king. To the east he fought savage wars against the heathen Saxons and the Avars who lived on the Hungarian plains. He defeated them with appalling cruelty and forcibly converted them to Christianity. To the south-west, he successfully stopped the Muslims from coming north of the Pyrennees. Charlemagne was looked on as the protector of Christian Europe, and in 800 the grateful pope crowned him Roman Emperor.

THE EARLY MONASTERIES

In the middle of the 6th century St Benedict of Nursia drew up a new rule, or scheme of organization, for monasteries. In time many monasteries followed it. They became better organized and the old jumble of churches and huts was replaced by well laid out cloisters, dormitories, *refectories* (where the monks ate), kitchens, and *scriptoria* (writing rooms). Nearby were the workshops and farm buildings, and the monks farmed the land around. The rule said that the monks should provide all they needed from the monastery and its lands.

Monasticism, or the coming together of men (and of women in a nunnery) were very important in the Middle Ages. Monasteries acted as inns and hospitals, they cared for the poor, they had almost the only libraries, and until the universities began to grow in the 12th century they and the cathedrals were the main centres of learning.

Part of a letter written by Alcuin of York. He was one of many scholars whom Charlemagne invited to his court at Aix (Aachen). Alcuin helped to develop a new kind of small letter, known as the Carolingian miniscule.
Right: A 9th-century bronze statue of Charlemagne on his horse.
Below: The 11th-century monastery of St Andrew at Chartres.

DIVIDING THE EMPIRE

By Frankish custom, a man's property was divided between his sons. When Charlemagne died his only living son, Louis the Pious, inherited all his lands. When Louis died, however, he had three living sons, Lothar, Lewis, and Charles. They were already fighting over their shares of his land. In 843 they reached a settlement. Charles took West Francia, or France. Lewis took Franconia, Saxony, Bavaria and the rest of Charlemagne's empire east of the Rhine. Between their lands lay the rich Middle Kingdom. This, and the title of Emperor, went to the eldest son Lothar. It included Charlemagne's lands in Italy and his capital at Aachen (Aix).

When Lothar died, his lands were again divided. The Frankish lands in Italy and the title of emperor eventually went, with the pope's support, to a German king. The rest of the Middle Kingdom had no natural boundaries. Kings of France to the west and Germany to the east tried to take over these lands and towns by gaining the loyalty of the great nobles and churchmen who ruled them.

This map shows how Charlemagne's empire was divided up between his grandsons.

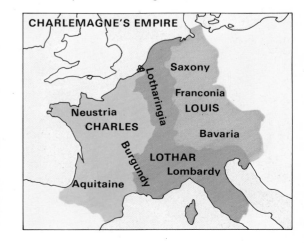

CHARLEMAGNE'S EMPIRE

Neustria
CHARLES
Saxony
Franconia
LOUIS
Lotharingia
Bavaria
Burgundy
LOTHAR
Lombardy
Aquitaine

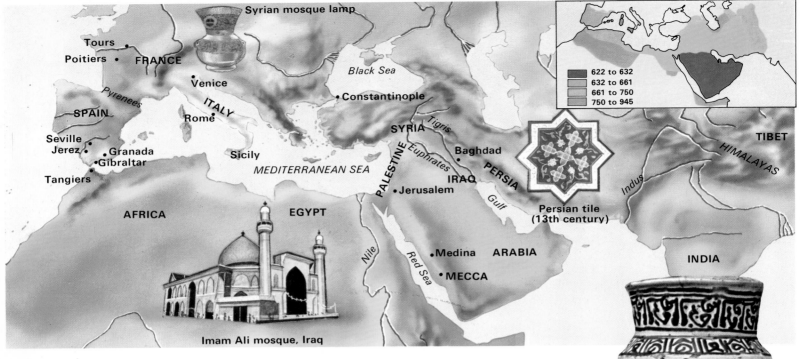

Syrian mosque lamp

Tours
Poitiers
FRANCE
Venice
Pyrenees
ITALY
SPAIN
Rome
Seville
Jerez
Granada
Gibraltar
Tangiers
AFRICA
EGYPT
MEDITERRANEAN SEA
Sicily
Black Sea
Constantinople
SYRIA
Tigris
Euphrates
PALESTINE
Baghdad
PERSIA
IRAQ
Jerusalem
Gulf
Nile
Red Sea
Medina
MECCA
ARABIA
Persian tile
(13th century)
Indus
TIBET
HIMALAYAS
INDIA

622 to 632
632 to 661
661 to 750
750 to 945

Imam Ali mosque, Iraq

The Spread of Islam

In the 7th century AD a new religion was founded in Arabia. It was known as *Islam*, which meant 'submission to the Will of Allah (God)'. Its followers were called *Muslims*. They wanted to spread their faith as widely as possible and within less than a hundred years they ruled an empire which stretched from Spain east to the borders of India.

Over the centuries the Muslims gained more and more land from the Byzantine empire. They threatened Christian Europe a number of times. In France Charles Martel defeated them near Poitiers in 732; his grandson Charlemagne fought them in the Pyrenees and, at sea, in the Mediterranean. For a time they controlled Sicily and even raided the suburbs of Rome in 846. From the 11th to the 13th centuries the Christians mounted Crusades to gain control of the Holy Land from them, but eventually they were unsuccessful. In the year 1453, the Muslim Ottoman Turks finally captured the last lands held by the Byzantine empire.

A tribal battle among Arabs. They were skilled fighters, specialising in surprise attacks from the desert. Then they would retreat into it, knowing few enemies could follow them there.

This drug jar, made in Spain in the 15th century, is decorated with Arabic writing. Muslims ruled much of Spain from the 8th to the 15th centuries.

THE PROPHET MUHAMMAD

Muhammad, the founder of Islam, came from Mecca in Arabia. It was then a trading town surrounded by desert, in which lived Bedouin tribes who moved from oasis to oasis with their flocks and herds.

Muhammad was born in AD 571. Muslims believe that when he was about 40 the angel Gabriel appeared to him as the messenger of Allah (God). Little by little he dictated to Muhammad Allah's commands, guidance for everyday life, warnings about Hell and promises about Paradise. Muhammad learned them by heart and repeated them to his followers. Later they were collected into a single book, the *Koran*. The language of the Koran is Arabic. Muhammad's own sayings are called *hadith*, the Traditions.

When Muhammad first preached Allah's message in Mecca, many people did not believe it. In 622 he went to Medina, another Arabian town. His journey is known as the Flight, or *Hijra*. Muslims saw it as the start of a new age and count their years from it. So 622 is the Muslim year 1. Muhammad gained many followers and his power grew. In 630 he went back to Mecca, this time as its ruler. In 632 (the Muslim year 11) he died, but his message lived and was spread by his followers.

Spreading the Faith

When Muhammad, the Prophet, died in 632 a great period of conquest began. Muslim warriors on horses and camels moved north to attack the Byzantine empire. Within 10 years of the Prophet's death Syria, Palestine and Egypt were in Arab hands. The Muslims moved westwards through North Africa, and eastwards to conquer Iraq, Persia and Afghanistan. As they went, they spread their faith. Often the local people welcomed them, for the rule of the Byzantine Christians had been very unpopular. Millions of people became Muslims, until they far outnumbered the Arabs. Many Christians and Jews were not willing to be converted. Muslim rulers usually left them in peace.

The first *caliphs*, or rulers, were all Arabs. Later, power passed to the Turks. They were originally nomads who had moved into Islamic areas from Central Asia, been converted and risen to immense power. Their story is told on page 56.

The Court of the Lions in the palace of the Alhambra at Granada in Spain. It was the last Muslim stronghold in Spain.

THE ARABS IN SPAIN

In 711 the second period of Islamic conquest began when Muslims crossed into Spain. They were led by the governor of Tangier. His name was Tarik and the huge rock at the southern tip of Spain was named Jebel al Tarik after him. We know it as Gibraltar. Soon much of Spain and Portugal was in Arab hands. They were prevented from conquering France by Charles Martel in 732.

Muslim farmers who knew about irrigation were able to cultivate vast new areas of Spain. For the first time, bananas, oranges, cotton, rice and sugar cane could be grown there. Vines from Persia were planted at Jerez de la Frontera, which gave its name to the *sherry* made from their grapes. Enough food was grown to provide for a large population.

Bit by bit, Muslim Spain was conquered by Christians from the north. The last Muslims were driven from Granada in 1492.

TRADE

The Islamic empire made trading in the Near East much easier and less dangerous than it had been in earlier times. Goods could be carried throughout the whole vast empire without ever crossing a single hostile frontier. A single kind of gold coin, the *dinar*, was used all through the empire.

Many goods were carried by sea. The Muslims imported wood from India and from Venice in exchange for gold which they got from West Africa, Arabia, eastern Europe and even Tibet. Other goods were carried overland by camels, donkeys, mules or horses roped together in small processions called *caravans*.

Products such as glass and cloth from Syria were spread through Islamic lands. So was sugar, grown first in Iraq and then in Egypt. Spices were a very profitable trade. Cloves, peppercorns, ginger and other spices from the Far East were brought to Tibet by Chinese merchants. There they traded them with the Arabs.

This picture, painted in Baghdad in 1237, shows travellers arriving in a village.

CHRONOLOGY
571	Muhammad is born in Mecca
610	Muhammad has his first revelation
622	Muhammad moves to Medina (the Hijra)
630	Muhammad returns to Mecca
632	Death of Muhammad
633	Muslims conquer Syria, Iraq, Egypt and Persia (to 640)
711	Muslims invade Spain and the Indus Valley
732	Muslims are defeated by the Franks at Poitiers
762	Baghdad becomes the Muslim capital
1055	Muslim Seljuk Turks seize Baghdad
1096	The First Crusade

The World in 800

Most of western Europe is now ruled by the Frankish king, Charlemagne, who is crowned Emperor by the pope in 800. To the north, the Vikings raid and colonize. In the Near East the Muslims gain lands from the Byzantine empire, and spread their rule to the borders of India. Hindu civilization expands outside India, and China becomes increasingly rich through trade. In the Americas, the Toltecs build an empire in Mexico and farther south the Maya civilization is at its height.

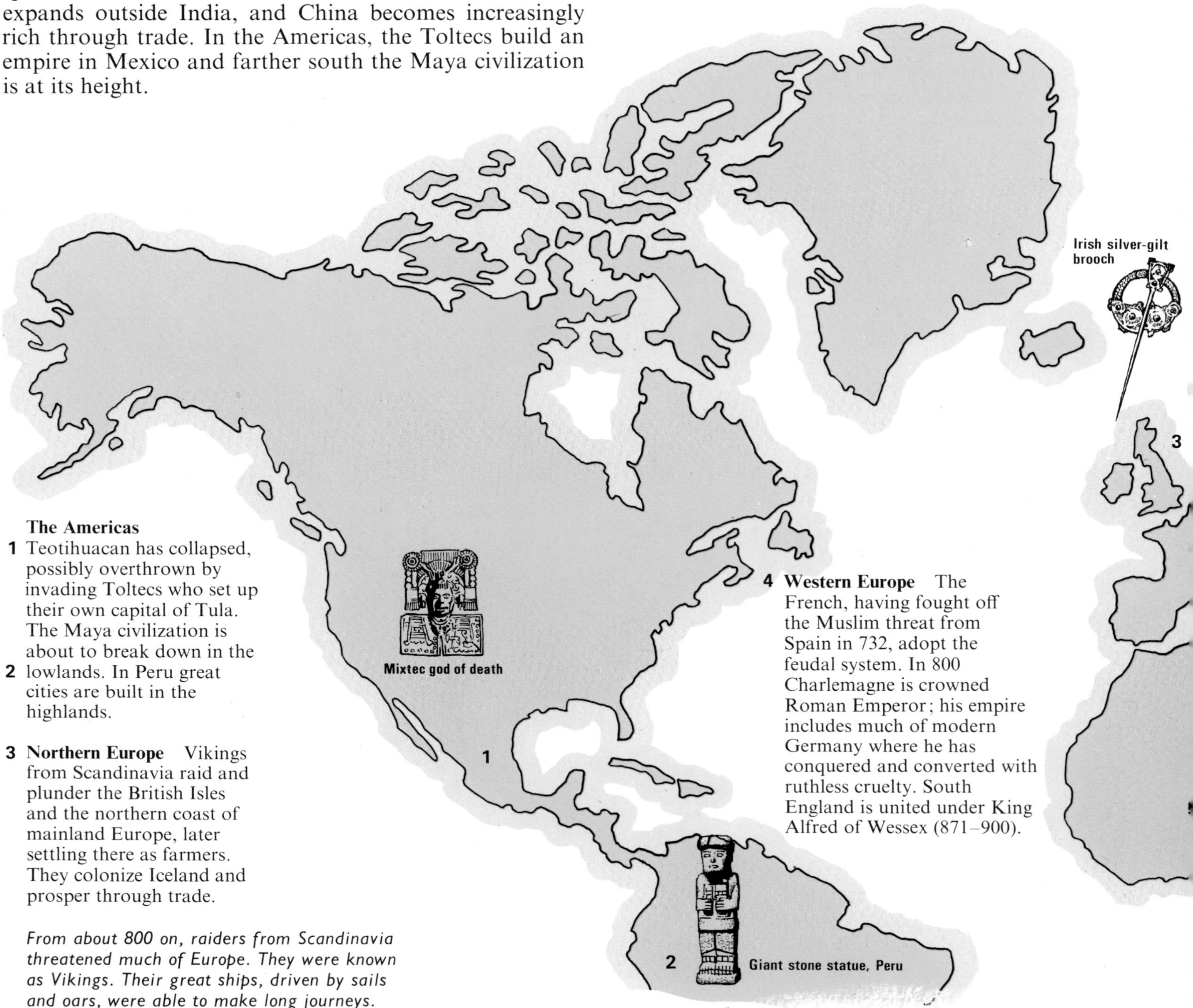

Irish silver-gilt brooch

3

The Americas

1 Teotihuacan has collapsed, possibly overthrown by invading Toltecs who set up their own capital of Tula. The Maya civilization is about to break down in the

2 lowlands. In Peru great cities are built in the highlands.

Mixtec god of death

3 **Northern Europe** Vikings from Scandinavia raid and plunder the British Isles and the northern coast of mainland Europe, later settling there as farmers. They colonize Iceland and prosper through trade.

From about 800 on, raiders from Scandinavia threatened much of Europe. They were known as Vikings. Their great ships, driven by sails and oars, were able to make long journeys. The Vikings were not just raiders, but also settlers and traders. They founded colonies from North America to Russia.

4 **Western Europe** The French, having fought off the Muslim threat from Spain in 732, adopt the feudal system. In 800 Charlemagne is crowned Roman Emperor; his empire includes much of modern Germany where he has conquered and converted with ruthless cruelty. South England is united under King Alfred of Wessex (871–900).

2 Giant stone statue, Peru

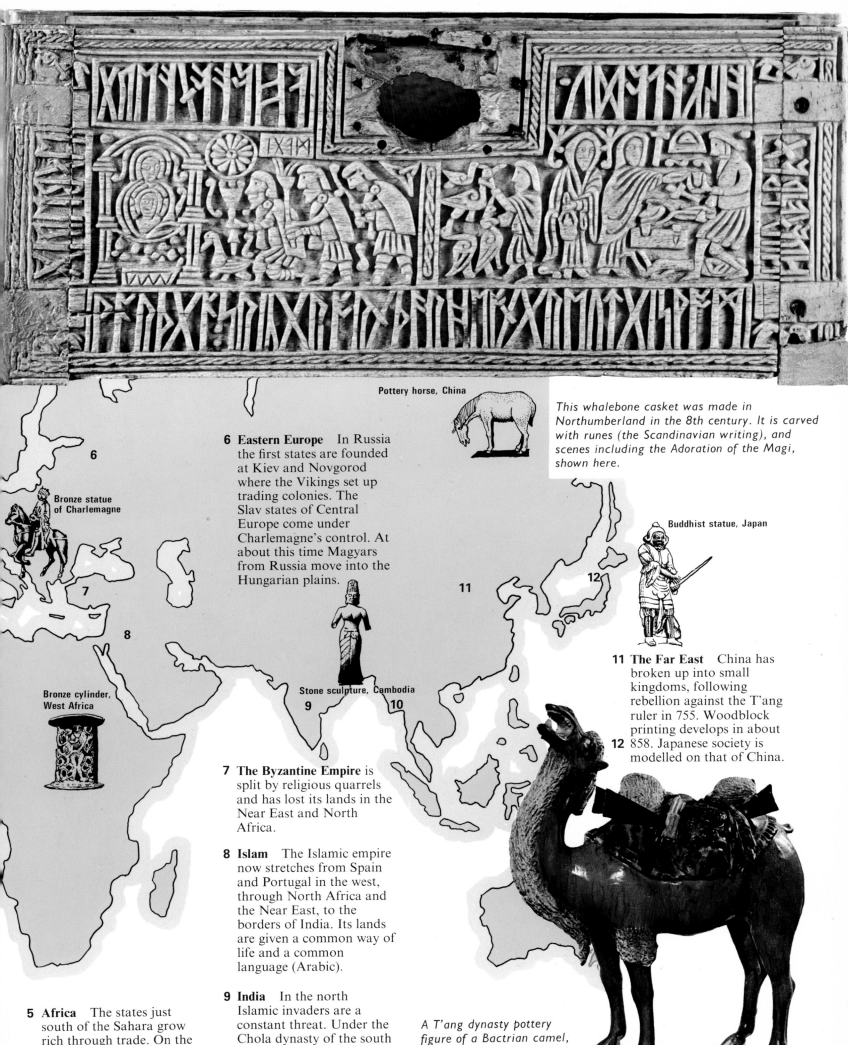

Pottery horse, China

6 Eastern Europe   In Russia the first states are founded at Kiev and Novgorod where the Vikings set up trading colonies. The Slav states of Central Europe come under Charlemagne's control. At about this time Magyars from Russia move into the Hungarian plains.

This whalebone casket was made in Northumberland in the 8th century. It is carved with runes (the Scandinavian writing), and scenes including the Adoration of the Magi, shown here.

Bronze statue of Charlemagne

Buddhist statue, Japan

Bronze cylinder, West Africa

Stone sculpture, Cambodia

11 The Far East   China has broken up into small kingdoms, following rebellion against the T'ang ruler in 755. Woodblock printing develops in about
12 858. Japanese society is modelled on that of China.

7 The Byzantine Empire is split by religious quarrels and has lost its lands in the Near East and North Africa.

8 Islam   The Islamic empire now stretches from Spain and Portugal in the west, through North Africa and the Near East, to the borders of India. Its lands are given a common way of life and a common language (Arabic).

9 India   In the north Islamic invaders are a constant threat. Under the Chola dynasty of the south
10 Hinduism is taken to Burma and Sumatra.

5 Africa   The states just south of the Sahara grow rich through trade. On the east coast Muslims build trading ports.

A T'ang dynasty pottery figure of a Bactrian camel, laden with Chinese goods for trading abroad.

23

The Vikings

BAFFIN IS.
GREENLAND
Silver coin (9th century)
ICELAND
ATLANTIC OCEAN
Prow of Viking longboat
Oak carving for ceremonial wagon
NORWAY
SWEDEN
Baltic Sea
Novgorod
RUSSIA
Volga
North Sea
DENMARK
BRITAIN
York
Dublin
Kiev
London
CARPATHIANS
Dnieper
Rouen
Paris
Black Sea
Alps
FRANCE
Constantinople
Rome
SPAIN
MEDITERRANEAN SEA
Seville

From the late 8th to the 11th centuries the people of northern Europe were terrified by raiders from the sea. They called them by different names. To the Anglo-Saxons they were 'Northmen' and Danes. The Germans called them *arcomanni*, the ship-men and the Arabs of Spain called them the heathen, *el-Majus*. Now we call them the Vikings.

The Vikings came from Scandinavia – what is now Norway, Sweden and Denmark. In those days they all spoke the same language and they moved freely from one region to another. Men from all over Scandinavia would join the warband of a chief who was known to be generous to his men. Scandinavians who went raiding were known as Vikings. We do not know just what this word means. It might have meant a man from a camp, or *wic*, or a man from a creek or *vik*. Perhaps it came from the word *vikja* which meant to go fast, or leave home.

The Vikings probably left their homes in search of farmland. Much of Scandinavia is mountainous or heavily forested, and only a tiny percentage of the land in Norway and Sweden could be farmed. Denmark provided better land where crops could be grown, as well as grazing land. Eventually there was not enough land to grow food for the increasing population, so many Scandinavians sailed away to set up colonies in Iceland, Greenland and eastwards in Russia. Others raided and looted the coasts of France and the British Isles. Here too many of them settled, buying land, marrying local women and turning from raiders to farmers.

In this Norwegian fjord, as in many others, the mountains drop sharply into the water. The only farmland lies at one end. The lack of land for growing food was one reason for the Vikings' raids and settlements.

CHRONOLOGY	
789	First Viking attacks on England
830s	Vikings found Dublin
834	Vikings raid Netherlands
850	Swedes begin to settle in East Baltic and Russia
860	Discovery of Iceland; Norwegians settle in British Isles
886	Danes allowed to settle in eastern England
911	Vikings settle in Normandy
986	Eirik the Red founds colony in Greenland
1003	Leif Eiriksson lands in North America
1066	Duke William of Normandy kills King Harold of England and becomes King William I of England

Raiders and Farmers

The first Viking raids on England came at the very end of the 8th century. Their ships appeared without warning. A large raiding band might have 400 men though they usually came in small bands of 60 or so. They demanded money and valuable goods from monasteries and towns, and if they did not get them they looted and plundered. Most accounts of Viking raids come from Christian monks who were appalled by their actions, specially because monasteries were holy places and were usually left unharmed.

The Vikings were not just raiders. They used some of their plunder to buy land. Vikings from Norway settled in the Scottish islands, around York in north-east England and in Ireland. The Danes were allowed to settle in eastern England and London, where their settlement had a Danish name, the Strand. King Alfred of Wessex stopped them spreading south-westwards.

The Vikings first visited mainland Europe as traders. But from the mid-9th century on they rowed up the great rivers to attack towns including Rouen and Paris. They were given huge amounts of silver to leave the towns in peace. In 911 the Viking chief Rollo was allowed to settle with his followers in what is now Normandy.

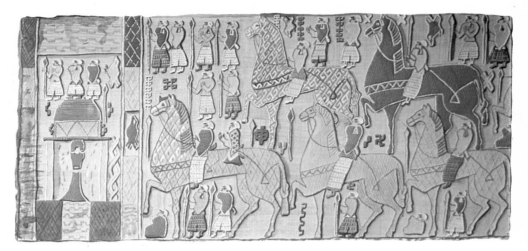

Part of a reconstruction of a tapestry found on the Oseberg ship, in which a Viking queen was buried in the 9th century.

TRADERS WITH THE EAST

While Danes and Norwegians explored western Europe, Swedes made their way along the great rivers to the east. They used small boats which could be carried overland from one river to another, which meant that they could travel eastwards down the river Volga to Bulghar and down the Dnieper to the Black Sea and Constantinople. They met traders from the Near East and from distant China. The Swedes set up two large colonies at Novgorod and Kiev. They were known as the *Rus*, from which comes our word Russia. They collected furs, amber, tar, wax, and slaves which they exchanged for luxuries including amethysts from Arabia, glass from Persia and Syria, spices from India, and silk cloth from China.

NEW LANDS IN THE WEST

The search for new farmlands took the Vikings on long voyages. Iceland was discovered some time before 900 and farming settlements grew up there. Families from Norway set off with their possessions and animals, including horses, sheep and goats. They travelled in open boats. The direct journey to Iceland took at least seven days with a good wind. It might take much longer if conditions were poor. Despite its name, Iceland is not terribly cold, and round the coasts the settlers found good grazing for their cattle. Sheep could graze on the poorer uplands. A little barley was grown. Fish and seabirds' eggs added to the food supply. The Iceland colonies did well. They set up their own national assembly, the *Althing*. Life there was less difficult than at home in Norway.

In 986 Eirik the Red founded a colony in Greenland. In spite of its name, much of this vast island is covered with ice, but the settlers could graze their cattle and there were many animals, among them foxes, seals and caribou, which could be hunted for fur and meat. The settlers traded furs and hides, falcons and animal oil for the corn, iron, and timber they needed.

More timber came from North America. In 1001 Eirik the Red's son Leif set out to find some lands to the west of Greenland which had been seen by sailors lost in fog. He found a rocky coast, perhaps part of Baffin Island. He landed there and then sailed south to what sounds like Labrador, which he named *Markland* or Wood Land, after its forests. He and his crew spent the winter in what may have been Newfoundland, which he called *Vinland* or Pasture Land. Poems and stories called *sagas* tell how the Vikings explored the North American coast, sailing perhaps as far south as Florida.

The Vikings never successfully colonized North America, although traders from Greenland went there for furs and timber until the mid-14th century. For the Greenland settlement was itself a failure. It was too far from Norway, on which the settlers depended for supplies. As the climate got colder and pack ice started to close the harbours, Eskimos attacked the settlers. Those who did not die abandoned the island.

This carving shows the legendary hero Sigurd killing the dragon Fafnir. Stories and poems about gods and heroes were learned by heart and handed down from one generation of storytellers to the next.

The Feudal Age

In the mid-8th century rulers like the Frank Charles Martel gave huge grants of land he owned or conquered to armed horsemen. In return, they swore an oath to fight for him when he asked them to. From this developed a whole system of government and way of life, based on land given and received in return for service and protection. It is known as the feudal system, because land given in this way was called a fief, or *feudum* in Latin.

Under the feudal system, the king granted land to great lords or tenants-in-chief. They in turn gave much of this land to tenants called knights, who would fight for them in return. When he was given his land the tenant (or vassal as he was called) swore an oath of loyalty to his lord. Below the knights came minor lords, farmers, and peasants. All received land and a great lord's protection, which was important in the early days when local fights or wars between great lords were quite common. In return they all provided services for their lords, whether by working on the land or by fighting for him.

In France and England the feudal system dominated life in the Middle Ages. It was never so important in Germany, but it spread eastwards to central and eastern Europe and there it lasted well into the 19th century.

In the Middle Ages great lords lived in castles. In times of war peasants from the surrounding countryside would come with their animals to shelter inside the castle's strong outer walls. Attackers would try many different ways to break into the castle. Great siege towers were wheeled up to the walls from which armed men could jump to the ramparts. Catapults hurled stones at the walls, and teams of men drove battering rams against them. The defenders shot arrows at the attackers, and dropped boiling oil and stones on to them. Often the attackers found they could not breach the walls, and then they camped round the castle, hoping the people inside would surrender for lack of food before help came.

CHRONOLOGY

1000s	Dykes and canals increase farmland in Flanders; forest is cleared in the Rhineland
1066	William of Normandy, King of England
1086	'Domesday Book' survey of England
1096	First Crusade
1154	Henry II, King of England; marries Eleanor of Aquitaine in France. He begins to give England a central government and a system of law
1180	Philip Augustus, King of France (to 1223); forces neighbours to acknowledge his overlordship
1205	King John of England has lost most of England's possessions in France
1215	Barons force John to seal Magna Carta limiting his rights over them
1226	Louis IX King of France (to 1270); growth of French 'parlement'
1265	Simon de Montfort summons English Parliament
1295	First truly representative English Parliament called by King Edward I
1316	Great famine in Europe, also in 1317
1337	Hundred Years' War (to 1453) between France and England
1346	English defeat French at Crecy
1348	The Black Death ravages Europe
1415	English defeat French at Agincourt
1429	Jeanne d'Arc raises English siege of Orleans; in 1431 she is burned as a relapsed heretic

LIFE ON THE LAND

At the bottom of the feudal 'pyramid' were the villeins, peasants who were tied to the place in which they were born. They were given strips of land in the village common fields, and in return they spent some time working on the lord's own fields. They might also have to pay the lord a sum of money each year, and give him some of their produce, such as corn, eggs, a lamb, and beeswax from their hives. They had to pay the lord a fee for having their corn ground in the lord's own mill.

The villagers' land was usually scattered in strips in the fields round the village, so that each villager had a share of good and bad land. Each field of many strips produced a crop such as wheat or barley, rye, oats, and some peas and beans, and every third year each field was left fallow (unplanted) so that the soil would recover its goodness. It was grazed by the villagers' sheep and pigs. Pigs could feed in the forest around, for in the Middle Ages there were far more forests than there are today.

FOOD

Ordinary peasants lived on coarse bread made from barley or rye flour, eggs, cheese, and milk, and on fruit and vegetables grown in their gardens. Sometimes they ate a chicken or a pig. Many trapped game, rabbits, and birds although this was against the law. Nobles ate much better food. Their bread was made from wheat flour, and they ate elaborate pastries with fruit soaked in honey. Meat was tough, and dishes were highly flavoured with spices such as pepper, mustard, and garlic. Most of the cattle had to be killed in the autumn or they would starve in the winter, and the meat was salted or pickled. In Lent, no one was allowed to eat meat, and fish were an important part of the diet.

This picture comes from a 15th-century book called 'Les Très Riches Heures du duc de Berry'. The Duke was a brother of King Charles V of France, and a great landowner. This picture shows work on the land in March.

England and France

Under the feudal system large landowners could become more powerful than the king who was their overlord. When Duke William of Normandy conquered England in 1066 he claimed all its land as his own. He tried to stop his main tenants-in-chief from gaining too much power by giving each of them land in several different regions. Even so, almost every English king had to deal with rebellious barons, as these great lords were known. Edward I (1272–1307) managed to set up a firm central government. He ruled with the help of a Parliament in which were knights and townsmen called burgesses, as well as the barons. The towns were outside the feudal system, and their burgesses were often opposed to the power of the great lords.

For a long time the king of France was almost powerless. In theory he was the overlord of several great dukes, among them the dukes of Normandy, Burgundy, and Aquitaine. In practice the king only controlled his personal lands, a relatively small area between Paris and Orleans. If the dukes refused to take their oath of loyalty to him, he could not force them to do so. After 1100 the French kings began to build up a system of government. They employed paid officials from the *bourgeoisie*, the townspeople who as in England were outside the feudal system. King Philip Augustus (1180–1223) used the fortune built up by efficient government to hire soldiers. He gained control of Normandy, Anjou, and Maine from King John of England, and strengthened his power over other great vassals (tenants). From then on the French king was a true power in the land.

THE BLACK DEATH

The worst and most famous outbreak of disease in the Middle Ages is known as the Black Death. The disease was bubonic plague, and it was spread by fleas from the black rats which often lived on ships. Almost everyone who caught the plague died from it.

In 1348 rats on ships from the East brought the plague to Europe. All countries were affected by it and probably over a third of the people in Europe died. Whole communities were wiped out, houses lay empty and derelict, and fields were overgrown.

The weather in Europe seems to have got worse in the 14th century. Winters lasted longer and summers were cold and wet. There were great famines when crops failed and animals died. When the Black Death struck, many people were too weak to resist it.

The results of the Black Death were felt at once. Food became dearer because fewer people were working on the land. Peasants began to demand freedom from the feudal system and better wages. Revolts by peasants broke out all over Europe, bringing feudal society to an end.

One of the greatest vassals of the French king was the king of England. When Duke William of Normandy conquered England in 1066 he kept his lands in France. Marriages brought more French land to the English kings until they controlled far more of France than the French kings. There were many wars between the two countries. They culminated in the Hundred Years' War which lasted (with lulls in the fighting) from 1337 to 1453. At first England gained great victories, but just when it looked as though France could never recover the peasant girl Jeanne d'Arc (Joan of Arc) brought new heart to the French. By 1453 the English had lost almost all their lands in France.

The World in 1000

By now most of north-western Europe has developed the feudal system of land granted in return for service. The Church plays a very important part in everyday life, and there are conflicts between popes and Holy Roman emperors who resent Church power and interference. In 1095 Pope Urban calls for the First Crusade against the Muslim rulers of the Holy Land. In the Islamic world the Arabs are losing power to the Turks, and in Africa the empire of Ghana falls to the Muslims in 1075.

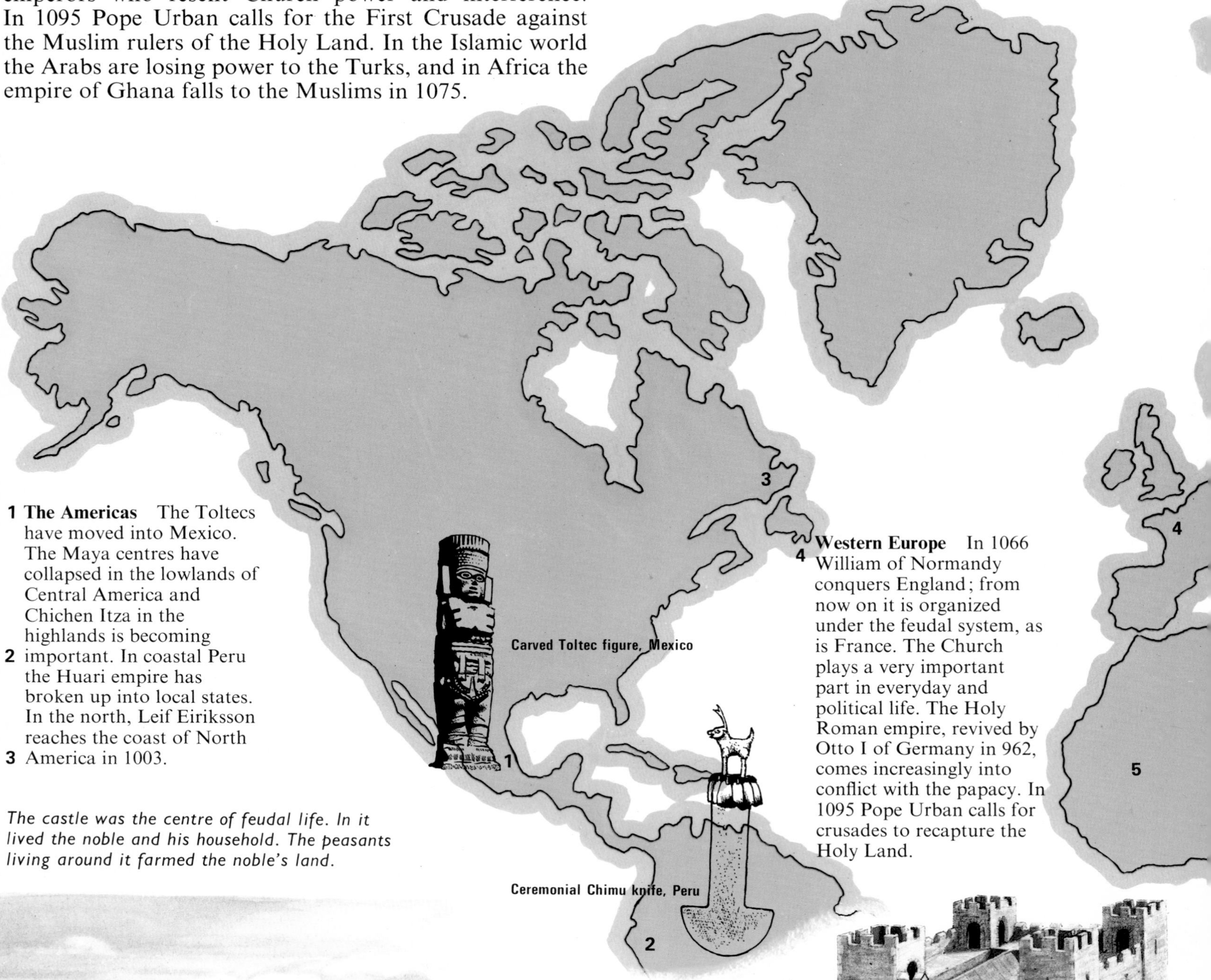

1 The Americas The Toltecs have moved into Mexico. The Maya centres have collapsed in the lowlands of Central America and Chichen Itza in the highlands is becoming **2** important. In coastal Peru the Huari empire has broken up into local states. In the north, Leif Eiriksson reaches the coast of North **3** America in 1003.

The castle was the centre of feudal life. In it lived the noble and his household. The peasants living around it farmed the noble's land.

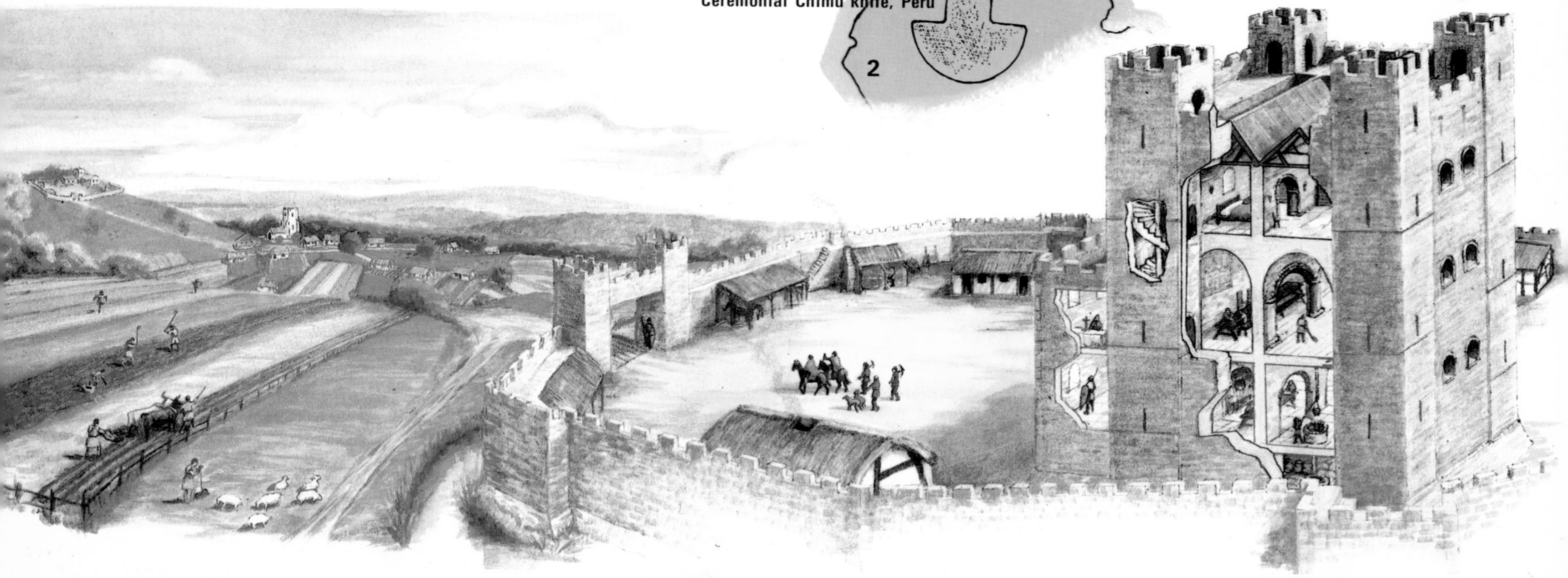

Carved Toltec figure, Mexico

Ceremonial Chimu knife, Peru

4 Western Europe In 1066 William of Normandy conquers England; from now on it is organized under the feudal system, as is France. The Church plays a very important part in everyday and political life. The Holy Roman empire, revived by Otto I of Germany in 962, comes increasingly into conflict with the papacy. In 1095 Pope Urban calls for crusades to recapture the Holy Land.

The Abbey of Cluny in Burgundy, on the borders of France and Germany in the old Middle Kingdom. Founded in 910, the Abbey followed the Benedictine rule. It was famous for the beauty of its services. A succession of strong abbots built up a great network of priories which obeyed the customs and example of Cluny.

6 Eastern Europe Vladimir of Kiev is converted to Byzantine Christianity in 988. Novgorod is now independent and Christian. The Magyars have settled the Hungarian plains and St Stephen centralizes government and introduces Christianity. Slavs in the Vistula plain have founded the Polish nation and are converted to Christianity.

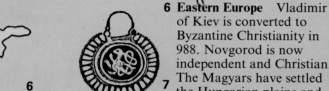
Silver earring from Kiev, Russia

Near Eastern bronze mosque lamp

Bronze statue of Shiva, India

Ceramic bowl, China
10

Japanese pagoda

A carved ivory box from 10th-century Islamic Spain.

Ife terracotta head, West Africa

9 The Byzantine Empire In 1071 Anatolia (modern Turkey) falls to the Seljuk Turks, and the Byzantine lands in Italy and Sicily are taken by the Normans. Only Constantinople and lands in the Balkans remain in its possession.

10 Far East In 960 the Sung dynasty unifies China. Printing spreads and textiles and porcelain, iron and steel are important industries. In Cambodia Angkor Thom becomes the Khmer capital. Burma is united and Buddhism becomes its main religion.

5 Africa The kingdom of Ghana, south of the Sahara, is converted to Islam. In about 1100 building of Greater Zimbabwe begins.

12 India Northern India is attacked by Muslims from the west, who loot and destroy. In the south the Hindu Chola kingdom has grown and is also gaining power in Ceylon.

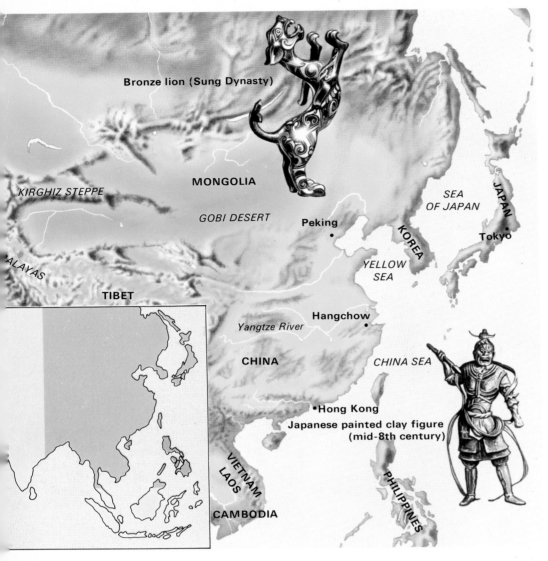

Bronze lion (Sung Dynasty)

KIRGHIZ STEPPE

MONGOLIA

GOBI DESERT

Peking

SEA OF JAPAN

JAPAN

Tokyo

KOREA

YELLOW SEA

HIMALAYAS

TIBET

Hangchow

Yangtze River

CHINA

CHINA SEA

Hong Kong

Japanese painted clay figure (mid-8th century)

VIETNAM

LAOS

PHILIPPINES

CAMBODIA

This picture of the West Lake near the great city of Hangchow was painted in the 13th century. The lake was a famous beauty spot, and feasts and entertainments were held on the boats and in the island restaurants. At this time Hangchow was the largest and richest city in the world.

China and Japan

China is the third largest country in the world and takes up the major part of mainland East Asia. It includes every sort of country, from deserts in the west to lush tropical forests, and from high mountains to flat river plains. In the north wheat is generally the main crop, while in the wetter and warmer south rice is most important.

Off the coast of northern East Asia is the cluster of islands which forms Japan. These islands are very mountainous, and in some places winters are cold with plenty of snow. There are good harbours along the coasts and the Japanese are skilled fishermen. Inland, wheat and rice are grown on the plains of the larger islands and on terraces up the mountainsides.

Chinese civilization was well developed long before cities grew up in Japan. As a result of this, Chinese influence on Japanese ways of life has been very strong.

CHRONOLOGY	
552	Buddhism reaches Japan
618	T'ang Dynasty in China (to 907)
624	Buddhism becomes established religion of Japan
645	All land in Japan comes under imperial control
751	Chinese armies in Central Asia are defeated by Arabs
907	End of T'ang Dynasty is followed by civil war until 960. Mongols begin capture of parts of northern China
939	Civil wars begin in Japan
960	Sung Dynasty in China (to 1279)
995	Japanese literary and artistic golden age (to 1028)
c1000	Gunpowder perfected in China
1185	Kamakura period in Japan (to 1333)
1210	Mongols led by Genghis Khan invade China
1274	Mongols unsuccessfully attempt to invade Japan
1279	Sung Dynasty falls to Mongols
1368	Yuan (Mongol) Dynasty is overthrown; Ming Dynasty (to 1644)
1421	Peking capital of China

The T'ang dynasty

In AD 618 one of the greatest ages of Chinese history, art and learning began. This was the start of the rule of the T'ang family, or dynasty, which lasted until about 900 AD.

Everyday life in China at this time was still the same in many ways as it had been for centuries. Most of the people were farmers, living in small villages. During this period the population of China increased very much, and the taxes everyone paid brought large sums to the government. The cities grew rich and T'ang China became the greatest empire of its day. It was a splendid period for Chinese art. Porcelain making, painting, lacquer working, sculpting, and architecture all flourished. The old civil service entrance examinations were brought back at this time. All local officials were appointed by the central government, and were not simply the local aristocrats.

At this time the old religion of Taoism and the recently introduced Buddhism were both very important. Buddhist monasteries were centres of learning, and at the same time were used as public baths, inns, and even banks. Some of them had priceless collections of manuscripts, and the buildings themselves were decorated with wall paintings and sculptured figures.

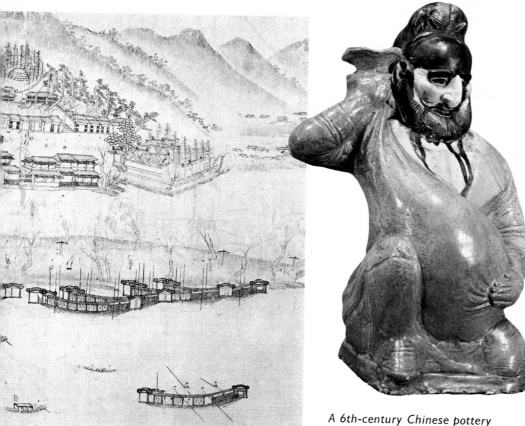

The Sung Dynasty

The Sung Dynasty was founded in 960 by a general called Chao K'uang-yin. He made China into a prosperous empire again. Habits, philosophies (ways of thought) and a general way of life became fixed in China during the Sung Dynasty. They changed hardly at all from then until quite modern times. One great invention of the Sung period was the abacus, an ancient calculator that is still used today. At the same time the custom began of binding the feet of upper-class girls to stop them growing. These 'lily feet', as they were called, crippled women for the rest of their lives.

Chao needed an enormous army of one and a quarter million men to protect his country against the barbarians in the north. This was a terrible drain on China's finances. In the end even this great army was no match for the invaders and in the 13th century all China was conquered by the Mongols.

A 6th-century Chinese pottery figure of an Armenian trader. He would have travelled along the Silk Road, the long caravan route that led from China, across Central Asia, to the Black Sea. From there Chinese goods were taken to Europe. Silk could be sold for a high price in the West because for a long time only the Chinese knew how to make it. It was the most valuable of all China's exports. Other important goods to come from China were porcelain, salt, tea, and spices. The Chinese usually employed middlemen to carry out their foreign trade.

The steep slopes of this Japanese island have been terraced so that food can be grown on them.

JAPAN

In the early centuries AD Japanese life was based on a clan system. Family groups called *Uji* each had a chief, and a kind of totem god thought to be an ancestor. In the 5th century the Yamato uji became the most important clan in southern Japan. Its chiefs are thought to be the ancestors of the emperors of Japan. Government in Japan was modelled as closely as possible on that of the T'ang rulers in China. Styles of building and even court rituals came from China too.

In the Middle Ages at least half of Japan was public land. Wealthy land-owners owned the rest in large estates and a feudal system grew up. Warrior nobles called *bushi* and *samurai* became very powerful. They fought with bows and arrows and their magnificant curved swords were made of the finest steel in the world. The leader of one warrior family, who was given the title of *shogun*, became more important than the emperor. He and his successors paid great respect to the emperor but they held the power. They were able to fight off two great invasions by China and Korea in the 13th century.

The 15th century was a time of great luxury and extravagance at the Japanese court but it was also a time of terrible civil war. Great landowners and warrior clans devastated the countryside and peasants starved or became bandits. Bands of pirates raided along the coasts. Japan did not recover until the middle of the 16th century.

THE VOYAGES OF CHENG HO

Between 1405 and 1433 a Chinese explorer, Cheng Ho, made seven great voyages. Each expedition was very large; there were 62 ships on the first, carrying over 27,000 men. The largest ships were over 120 metres (400 feet) long, and 55 metres (180 feet) wide.

On each voyage the fleet called at Malacca on the Malay peninsula. Here traders from all over the East brought goods for exchange. Then the fleet split up. Some ships went to Java and Sumatra. Others went to Burma, India, Ceylon, and even westward to Hormuz on the Gulf. On his fifth voyage, which began in 1417, Cheng Ho reached Mogadisho on the east coast of Africa. Cheng Ho's ships carried Chinese porcelain, silks, gold and silver, iron and copperware. These were traded for spices and ivory, precious stones and dyes. But, unlike the Europeans later, the Chinese did not try to create colonies in India or Africa.

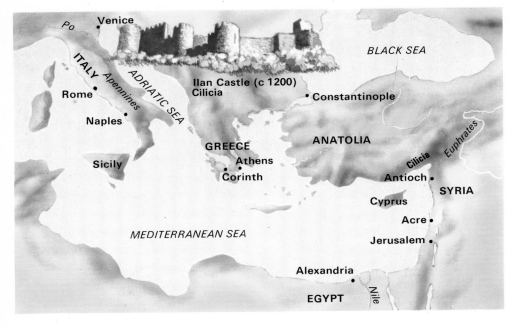

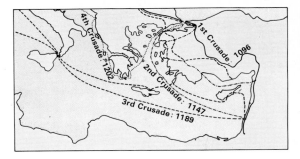

The Crusades

During the Middle Ages many Christians went as pilgrims to Jerusalem and the other Bible lands (the Holy Land). They believed that by going on this dangerous journey they might be forgiven their sins. From the 7th century the Holy Land had been ruled by the Muslim Arabs, but they had generally not interfered with the pilgrims. Then, in 1071, the Turks conquered much of the area. They put many pilgrims to death, and robbed and tortured others. They moved north to threaten the Christian Byzantine empire.

In November 1095 Pope Urban II preached a sermon calling on faithful Christians to journey to the Holy Land on a holy war or *crusade* (from the Latin word for cross) against the Turks. He said:

. . . an accursed race, a race wholly alienated from God . . . has violently invaded the lands of these Christians and has depopulated them by pillage and fire . . . Accordingly undertake this journey for the remission [forgiveness] of your sins, with the assurance of the imperishable glory of the kingdom of Heaven.

The First Crusade

All over Europe men began to raise armies to march to Jerusalem. Before the great lords had organized themselves, thousands of peasants and vagabonds, led by a monk nicknamed Peter the Hermit, made their way to Constantinople. The Byzantine emperor, whose appeal for help had led to Urban's sermon, was nervous of their strength and quickly sent them on to the Holy Land. Almost all of them were killed by the Turks.

By November 1096 a large army was gathering at Constantinople, led by great lords including Robert of Flanders, Stephen of Blois, Raymond of Toulouse, and Robert of Normandy. They led their soldiers on what we call the First Crusade. It was a great success. Antioch in Syria was captured in 1098 and Jerusalem fell in 1099. The Turks were driven from much of the Holy Land and a new kingdom of Jerusalem known as Outremer, 'the land beyond the sea', was set up.

Below: The siege of Jerusalem in 1099 lasted 40 days. When they finally captured the city, the Crusaders massacred the Muslims who had defended it and the Jews who lived there.

CHRONOLOGY	
1096	First Crusade begins
1099	Crusaders capture Jerusalem
1104	Crusaders capture Acre
1147	Second Crusade (ends 1149)
1174	Muslims under Saladin conquer Syria
1187	Saladin captures Jerusalem
1189	Third Crusade (ends 1192)
1191	Crusaders conquer Cyprus and capture Acre
1192	Richard makes peace with Saladin
1202	Fourth Crusade (ends 1204)
1204	Crusaders sack Constantinople
1217	Fifth Crusade (ends 1222)
1228	Sixth Crusade (ends 1229)
1248	Seventh Crusade (ends 1270)

005419

RICHES AND TRADE

Many of the crusaders were devout Christians, but some of them were more interested in gaining riches and even land for themselves. In the end, the crusades did most good to the trading cities of Italy, above all to Venice and Genoa, which gained money from transporting the crusaders in their ships and from setting up trade networks with the East.

The crusades brought knights from Europe into contact with the East. They returned with a taste for spices, such as ginger, pepper, and cinnamon; for new fruits such as dates and figs; and for comforts such as rugs for the floor and silk for clothes. Trade in all of these became very important.

CRUSADER STATES

Pope Urban II described Jerusalem as 'the centre of the Earth'. He said its land was 'fruitful above others like a paradise of delights'. This was an exaggeration, but there were fertile lands in and around the Holy Land. During the 11th and 12th centuries a number of states was set up there by European knights, most of whom had come to the area as crusaders.

In the 11th century the Normans set up a kingdom in south Italy, and in Sicily under Roger of Sicily and Robert Guiscard. The same year Robert's son Bohemond led a crusade which seized Antioch and Bohemond made himself its prince. Jerusalem itself was taken in 1099 after a siege and Godfrey of Bouillon was chosen as ruler over the new Christian conquests.

Although Byzantium was a Christian empire, the Norman crusaders, in particular, soon became hostile to it. In 1147 Roger of Sicily raided Greece and sacked Corinth. During the Third Crusade King Richard conquered Cyprus from the Byzantines and made Guy de Lusignan its king.

By the 13th century Count Baldwin of Flanders ruled at Constantinople, and there were French kingdoms in Cyprus, Athens, Thessaly, and Achaea. Although this French power seemed to be very great, in many places control was poor. Rulers were not united. This disunity helped the Byzantines to reclaim some lands and drive the conquerers away.

The castle of Krak des Chevaliers in Syria was built by the Knights of St John. It stood firm through 12 sieges before it fell in 1271. It was built on a cliff and within its strong outer walls were barracks, storerooms, and a windmill.

King Richard of England (above) and the Muslim leader Saladin (below), from a 13th-century tile. Richard defeated Saladin and marched within sight of Jerusalem. But he realized he could never capture the city and made peace.

The Later Crusades

The First Crusade had been a great success. But the Turks and Egyptians attacked the crusaders over and over again and began to win back the Holy Land. Several more crusades were called, and King Louis VII of France, Conrad III of Germany, and later Richard I of England, Philip Augustus of France, and Frederick Barbarossa of Germany all pledged themselves to recapture Jerusalem.

Illness and disaster prevented several expeditions from even reaching the Holy Land, and quarrels often broke out among the crusaders. Richard I captured Acre and came within sight of Jerusalem, but he realized he could never retake it. In 1203 the Venetians and the crusaders captured the Christian city of Constantinople. Although many Christians dreamed of recapturing Jerusalem, and many set out on crusades, they never succeeded.

The Crusaders land at Damietta in Egypt. They often travelled overland to the Near East, through the Balkans to Constantinople, and then south through Anatolia. Many went by sea, which was safer and healthier but took longer. In the 12th century two special orders of knights, the Knights Templar and Knights of St John of Jerusalem, were formed to aid and protect pilgrims to the Holy Land.

Eastern Europe

Along the northern edge of Europe, stretching from Belgium far eastwards to Russia, is a vast plain. Through it great rivers, the Rhine, the Weser, the Elbe, the Oder and the Vistula, run north to the North Sea and the Baltic. In the Middle Ages this area was largely covered with forest which settlers cleared to get fertile farmland. South of the plain rise the mountains of Bohemia and the Carpathians, and south again is the great Hungarian plain around the river Danube. The Rhine and Danube formed the eastern frontier of the Roman empire for several centuries.

In the Age of Migrations from the 3rd to the 8th centuries AD 'barbarian' tribes were moving through eastern Europe. Some moved south and west from the Baltic region, and others made their way westwards from Central Asia. They included the nomad Huns and Avars, and also the Slavs who had settled in much of eastern Europe by AD 600.

The 13th-century castle of Malbork, near Gdansk in Poland. It was the seat of the grand master of the Teutonic Knights from 1309 to 1457.

THE TEUTONIC KNIGHTS

In 1198 some German merchants joined together to help nurse the sick and look after pilgrims to the Holy Land. Ten years later they had become known as the Teutonic (German) Order of Knights. They worked under a monastic and military rule.

In 1226 the knights were invited to help a Polish duke defend his lands on the lower reaches of the river Vistula from the pagan Prussians. They colonized East Prussia and converted its people. The Order ruled East Prussia by setting up a series of military towns and using the local people ruthlessly to work on the land. They encouraged many German peasants to settle in the Prussian countryside. They farmed what had previously been wild land, from the lower Vistula and the Baltic coast to the southern borderland.

The knights grew more and more powerful until they controlled much of the Baltic coast. They quarrelled with the merchants of the growing Hanseatic ports (see page 48) and became increasingly unpopular. In 1410 the Poles and Lithuanians defeated the knights at Tannenburg. In 1466 the Order came under Polish rule.

Poland

In the 10th century AD the Slav tribes in the plains around the Vistula joined together under their leader Mieszko to form Poland. At this time Germans were moving eastward, converting the Slavs and settling the land. To safeguard their country, Mieszko and his people became Christians and acknowledged the overlordship of the Holy Roman emperor. In the next century Polish rule was pushed eastward to Kiev, but in 1138 King Boleslaw died and his kingdom was divided between his sons. Split into small states, Poland could barely defend itself against the invasions of the Mongols from Central Asia, or from its pagan neighbours Lithuania and Prussia. The Poles called in the Teutonic knights to help, and then found themselves faced by the powerful state of the knights in Prussia and Lithuania.

Gradually the Poles recovered their strength and unity. They were helped by many immigrants, who were peasants, traders and craftsmen from Germany, and Jews who had been expelled from almost every other country at this time. From 1370 to 1382 Poland was united with Hungary under King Louis I. After he died the Poles chose his daughter Jadwiga to be their Queen, and in 1386 she married Jagello, duke of Lithuania. The two countries were united. Jagello and the Lithuanians became Christians. In 1410 Jagello scored a great victory over the Teutonic knights, and he built Poland-Lithuania into the largest state in eastern Europe.

Hungary

In the 9th century AD the Magyars, a tribe from central Asia, settled in the Hungarian plains. Here, since Roman times, wheat and vines had been grown on the fertile soil around the Danube. The Magyars now raided deep into the rest of Europe. They were described as:

of a sickening ugliness. Their deepset eyes had an inhuman look; their heads seemed bald, but from their pates sprung thin pigtails. Their voices were frighteningly shrill, and their language was different from any human tongue. Like wild animals they devoured raw flesh and drank blood.

The Magyars were expert horsemen and raided as far west as central France and Italy. But in the mid-10th century they were defeated by the Germans in two great battles and then settled down in the Hungarian plains, with many Slav subjects. Not long after they became Christian.

The Magyars, or Hungarians as they became known, built up a large kingdom which was well organized on feudal lines. They were helped by wealth from rich gold and silver mines. But the position of their country meant that it was always in danger of attack from the east. In the mid-13th century it was ravaged by raids from the Mongols, who killed many people, and in the next century began a long series of struggles with the Turks.

Above: This Hungarian aquamanile (a vessel for carrying water for washing hands) dates from the 12th century. Below left: The crown of St Stephen, part of the Hungarian royal regalia. According to tradition, it was given to Stephen by the pope in recognition of his work converting pagans to Christianity. Taken by the Nazis in the Second World War, it came into American hands, and was returned to Hungary only in 1978.

Russia

The first states in Russia were set up by trading colonies of Vikings at Novgorod in the north and farther south at Kiev. In 988 Prince Vladimir of Kiev was converted to the Orthodox Christianity of the Byzantine empire.

Within about 50 years Kiev is said to have had some 200 churches, built and decorated in the Byzantine style (see page 15). Trade in furs, wax, slaves, and honey brought the state wealth. Other states grew up to the north, loosely ruled by Kiev.

Nomads from Central Asia were a constant threat to these states. In the 13th century the Mongols conquered much of Russia, burning down towns and killing many of the people. The people of Novgorod paid tribute to the Mongols but were not conquered by them. They later set up a republic. Trade was becoming more and more important in the Baltic area and Novgorod allowed the Hanseatic merchants to build a settlement there (see page 48).

Meanwhile the trading town of Moscow to the south-east was growing bigger and more important, although it was captured twice by the Mongols. Under Ivan the Great, at the end of the 15th century, it gained control of the surrounding states including Novgorod, and Ivan claimed to be Ruler of all Russia.

THE CENTRAL REGION

Modern Czechoslovakia is in the centre of eastern Europe. Much of the country is mountainous and covered with forests. It was formed in 1918 out of Bohemia in the west, Slovakia in the east, and Moravia in the middle. These countries were surrounded by powerful neighbours: Germany in the west, Poland to the north, Austria and Hungary in the south, and on the east Russia. They struggled for independence all through the Middle Ages. In the 10th century Slovakia was conquered by the Magyars, and from then on it was subject to the ruler of Hungary. Bohemia and Moravia formed a Christian kingdom, dominated sometimes by the Poles and sometimes by the Germans. From the 16th century they were ruled by the Hapsburg family who also ruled the Holy Roman Empire.

A Mongol camp in the Kirghiz mountains. Now, as in the Middle Ages, the Mongols live in felt tents called yurts, moving from winter pasture to summer pasture with their flocks and herds.

Mongol soldiers and their horses. The missionary John of Plano Carpini, who travelled through Mongol territory in the mid-13th century, wrote a description of the Mongol armies. Each soldier had three or four mounts, which they often changed. A soldier's weapons included two or three bows, three quivers of arrows, an axe, rope, and a sword.

The Mongols

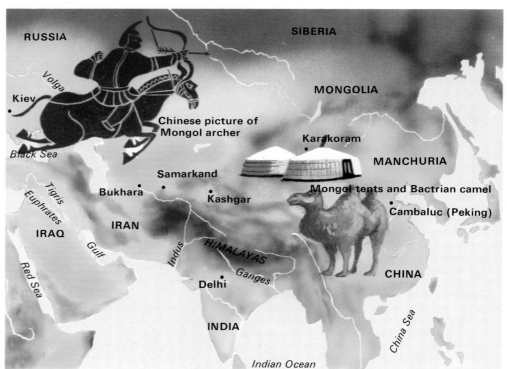

RUSSIA

SIBERIA

Kiev

Volga

Black Sea

Chinese picture of Mongol archer

MONGOLIA

Karakoram

MANCHURIA

Samarkand

Tigris

Euphrates

Bukhara

Kashgar

Mongol tents and Bactrian camel

Cambaluc (Peking)

IRAQ

Gulf

IRAN

Indus

HIMALAYAS

Ganges

CHINA

Red Sea

Delhi

China Sea

INDIA

Indian Ocean

Between north-west China and Siberia stretches a vast area of rolling grassland known as the Steppes. This is the homeland of a nomadic people called the Mongols. The early Mongols migrated with the seasons, taking their sheep and horses from one good pasture to another. Then as now, the Mongols were superb horsemen. This skill helped them to become unrivalled hunters and warriors. During the Middle Ages the Mongols built up an empire stretching from China to the borders of Hungary.

The First Empire

From ancient times Mongol tribes, greedy for the riches of the great Chinese cities to the south, would leave their bleak grasslands and attack them destroying everything in their path. In the 3rd century BC the Chinese built the Great Wall to keep them out, but in the end even this was not to prove successful.

By the middle of the 10th century AD Mongol tribes had built up an empire covering much of Manchuria, Mongolia and north-east China. The Mongols began to live in the cities they conquered, and used Chinese people to advise them in running the empire. They gradually adopted many Chinese customs. This group of Mongols was eventually overrun by another tribe from the west, but they mark the start of centuries of Mongol activity.

CHRONOLOGY

1206	Temujin elected Genghis Khan (to 1227)
1215	Peking falls to Genghis Khan who also moves west to Gulf and builds up a vast empire
1227	Genghis Khan's empire is divided into four Khanates
1238	Mongols annihilate Volga Bulgars and move on into Russia
1240	Kiev falls to Mongols
1241	Mongols ravage much of Hungary and Poland
1260	Kublai Khan makes Peking his capital
1274	Japanese fight off Mongol invasion
1279	Kublai Khan finally destroys Sung Dynasty
1360	Timur the Lame, Great Emir (to 1405)
1368	Mongols driven from Peking
1388	Mongol capital Karakoram destroyed by Chinese
1393	Timur captures Baghdad
1398	Timur destroys Delhi

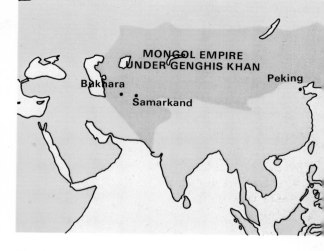

MONGOL EMPIRE UNDER GENGHIS KHAN
Bukhara · Samarkand · Peking

'THE VERY MIGHTY LORD'

Genghis Khan, the great leader who brought all the Mongol tribes under his control, was born in 1167. His name was Temujin. Soon after he became chief of his tribe he managed to win the support of many other Mongol leaders by his bravery and daring. In 1206 he took the title Genghis Khan, which means 'the very mighty lord'.

Genghis Khan led his Mongol horde all across Central Asia, raiding and plundering and capturing cities such as Bukhara and Samarkand. His warriors encircled their enemies with flying columns of horsemen, and their most important weapon was a heavy bow. The Mongols controlled their horses with their feet, so that their hands were free for fighting. Messengers using relays of horses could ride 400 kilometres (250 miles) in a day.

Genghis Khan was wise enough to use the skills of foreign craftsmen and specialists to help rule his empire. He was interested in travellers and missionaries, and traders were allowed to journey through his lands. However, he admitted that he found his greatest joy in conquest, victory and the glory of war.

The Four Khanates

When Genghis Khan died in 1227 his empire was divided up, according to tribal custom, between his four sons. The grandsons of the great Khan took the Mongol hordes to nearly every part of Asia, and deep into Europe. By the end of the 13th century four great Mongol kingdoms formed a 'superstate' stretching from the China Sea to the borders of Poland and Hungary.

These four Khanates, as they were called, were that of the Great Khan, including all of China and Mongolia; the Khanate of Chughtai centred around Kashgar, Samarkand, and Bukhara; the Khanate of Persia stretching from near the Indus river to the Black Sea; and the Khanate of Kipchak or the Golden Horde, which included Greater Russia as far east as Mongolia itself. However, the Mongols were better as conquerors than as rulers and settlers. After the devastating shock of conquest, local people were able to grow strong enough to drive them out.

Mongol soldiers, mounted on tough, stocky ponies, were almost unbeatable. They attacked with devastating speed and skill. At night they signalled their movements to one another with drums, horns, shouts, and even bird calls.

Trade

Trade went on busily during the Mongol empires, and contacts between China and the lands to the west increased very much. Travellers, merchants, and priests made journeys back and forth across Asia. To the west went trade goods of all kinds, including porcelain and silks, and technical knowledge such as the making of gunpowder. In return, Mongol converts took the religion of Islam back to parts of China.

The Italian Marco Polo visited the court of Kublai Khan at Cambaluc (Peking) in the late 13th century. He wrote a book describing his visit, which is the first accurate record of China by a European. For centuries his European readers could hardly believe the wonders he described.

The Last Great Leader

In the late 14th century, Timur the Lame rose to power in Samarkand. He overran Persia, Mesopotamia and the Golden Horde in south Russia, and devastated northern India. When he died in 1405 he was on his way to China to convert the Chinese to Islam. On his death, Mongol power in Central Asia was broken. With it went centuries-old links between East and West. The Mongols continued to be a great menace to the Chinese, but they never again controlled an empire. They went back to the old nomadic way of life they had known before.

The World in 1250

Mongols from central Asia take control of northern China, invade India, gain control of part of the Near East, and raid deep into Russia and central Europe. The Crusades have brought western Europe in close touch with the Islamic world and trade between them grows. Towns are growing large and wealthy through trade, weakening the feudal system with its reliance on lord and land. In some of them universities are growing up. In 1271 Marco Polo sets out from Italy for China, where the Sung capital of Hangchow is the richest city of the world. The Turks become increasingly important.

Right: Part of the Catalan map, made for the king of France in about 1375. Much of it was based on seamen's charts which since the late 13th century had been drawn up using compass bearings. They were more accurate than any other kind of medieval maps. The Catalan map's information on Central Asia and China came largely from the writings of Marco Polo.

Muslims and Christians in battle. At the end of the 11th century Pope Urban called on Christians to journey to the Holy Land and capture it from the Muslim Turks so that pilgrims could safely visit Jerusalem and other holy places. From then on there were a number of Crusades, as such expeditions were called. At first the Christians were successful, but the states they set up were soon recaptured by the Muslims and in 1291 they were finally driven out of the Holy Land.

Toltec temple at Tula, Mexico

Chimu decorated gold beaker, Peru

1 **The Americas** In coastal Peru the Chimu control a well organized state. In
2 Mexico the Mixtecs are established in the Valley of Oaxaca.

3 **Western Europe** In England and France strong central governments are set up. More land is cultivated. Trade grows, and towns become larger and richer. The conflict between the Empire and the Papacy continues and in northern Italy towns gain independence. Universities are founded. The Crusades have failed to win back the Holy Land.

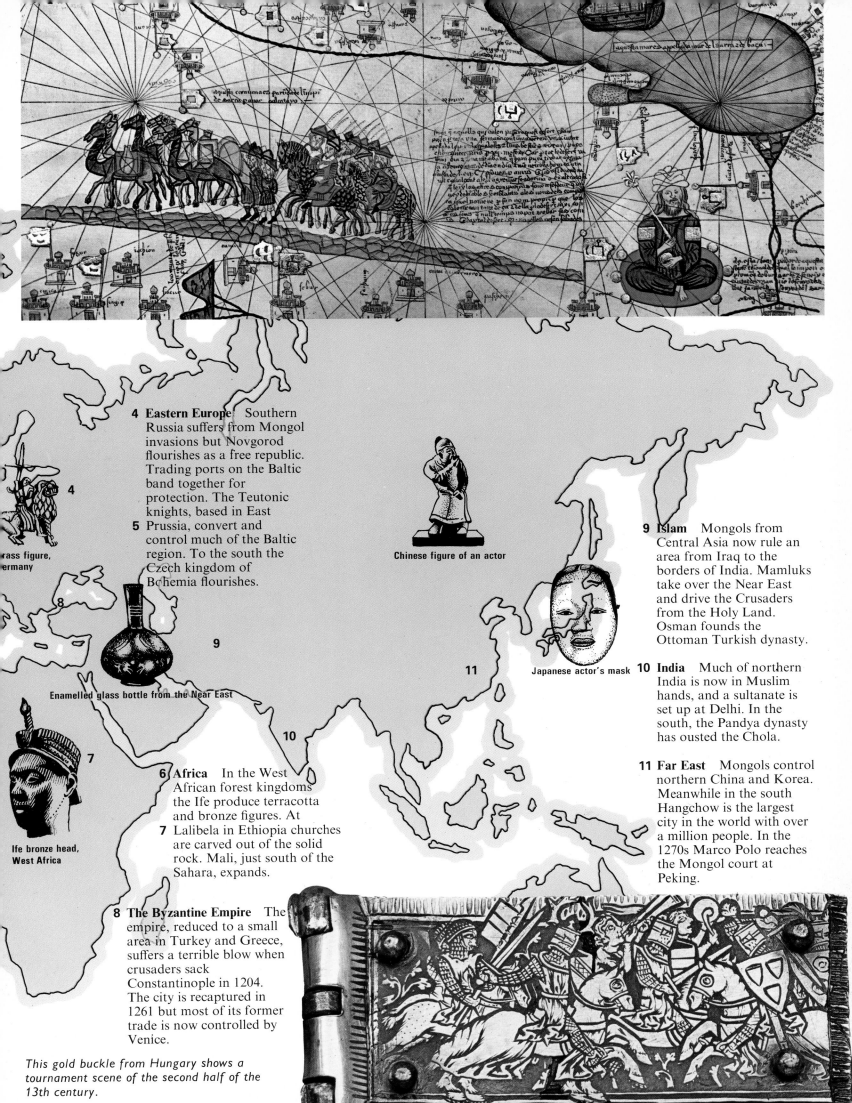

4 Eastern Europe Southern Russia suffers from Mongol invasions but Novgorod flourishes as a free republic. Trading ports on the Baltic band together for protection. The Teutonic knights, based in East

5 Prussia, convert and control much of the Baltic region. To the south the Czech kingdom of Bohemia flourishes.

Chinese figure of an actor

9 Islam Mongols from Central Asia now rule an area from Iraq to the borders of India. Mamluks take over the Near East and drive the Crusaders from the Holy Land. Osman founds the Ottoman Turkish dynasty.

rass figure, ermany

Japanese actor's mask

10 India Much of northern India is now in Muslim hands, and a sultanate is set up at Delhi. In the south, the Pandya dynasty has ousted the Chola.

Enamelled glass bottle from the Near East

11 Far East Mongols control northern China and Korea. Meanwhile in the south Hangchow is the largest city in the world with over a million people. In the 1270s Marco Polo reaches the Mongol court at Peking.

Ife bronze head, West Africa

6 Africa In the West African forest kingdoms the Ife produce terracotta and bronze figures. At

7 Lalibela in Ethiopia churches are carved out of the solid rock. Mali, just south of the Sahara, expands.

8 The Byzantine Empire The empire, reduced to a small area in Turkey and Greece, suffers a terrible blow when crusaders sack Constantinople in 1204. The city is recaptured in 1261 but most of its former trade is now controlled by Venice.

This gold buckle from Hungary shows a tournament scene of the second half of the 13th century.

Towns and Traders

A market scene in a French town of the Middle Ages. Town life became increasingly important with the growth of wealth and trade, and the towns had a good deal of independence within the feudal system.

Most Roman towns survived the fall of the empire, although they became smaller. In the 10th century rulers and great lords and churchmen founded many new towns, some for defence and others as market and administrative centres. Roads were very bad, and in general trade was carried out by sea and river. Trading towns grew up on coasts and river banks, fortified against attacks from raiders.

In the 11th and 12th centuries new lands were cultivated. People became richer and trade became more important. A new class of people grew up. These were the merchants.

New Allegiances

Merchants were not closely tied to the feudal system. Their lives were based on trade and money, not on land. Towns of merchants grew up which often owed allegiance not to the local lord, but to the king. A serf who lived in a town for a year and a day gained his freedom from the land. The townspeople were known as burgesses, burghers, or bourgeoisie, from the words *burg* or *bourg* meaning a fortified place.

Many of the fortified places round which the towns grew up were Church centres. Others began as trading settlements where roads crossed or a river could be forded. Some were founded by kings who realized that they would be useful as a balance to the power of the nobles. They promised good conditions to attract people and gain their allegiance. Nobles, too, founded towns in their own lands. This happened specially often on the eastern borders of Germany where new lands were being settled.

Some of the new towns grew very wealthy. They spent much of their money on defence, hiring soldiers and building strong walls to protect themselves against robbers and in times of war.

Great fairs grew up along the main trading thoroughfares. This 15th-century picture shows the fair at Lendit in France.

Roads and Fairs

Trade routes overland generally followed the old Roman roads, although they were now usually just made of gravel and mud. Traffic on them was very heavy. Rich people travelled on horseback but most people walked everywhere. Merchants loaded their goods on trains of pack animals and often travelled in convoys for safety. No one dared travel at night for fear of robbers, and along the roads were many inns and hostels.

Many trade fairs grew up along the routes. The roads from Flanders, Germany, Italy, and southern France crossed in the region of Champagne, which became famous for the great fairs held there every year. The six most important fairs lasted for 49 days each, and merchants from many countries met there. The last two weeks were spent in settling accounts. Goods at such fairs were tested for weight and quality, and special courts were set up to sort out disputes.

The Guilds

The main organization of a medieval town was the guild. At first this was an association of all the merchants in a town, who joined together to give one another help and protection. Later craft guilds were formed by the masters of a certain trade in a town. There were guilds of goldsmiths, leather-workers, fishmongers, carpenters, and so on. The guilds made rules about the way in which people worked, and how long they worked for. They set prices and said what was the most a workman could be paid. They limited the number of people who could work in a particular trade or craft, and cheats and anyone giving the trade a bad name were punished. This strict system made sure that standards were kept high, but it stopped new ideas from developing.

In many cities the guilds became very rich and powerful. They built guild halls where they could meet. They gave stained glass windows to cathedrals and parts of town churches were often set aside for their members to worship in.

A boy who wanted to join a guild spent several years as an apprentice, working for little but his food and lodging. At the end of a set time he had to show the guild that he knew his job. Then he entered the guild as a craftsman. If he did very well he could become a master craftsman, one of the chief men in the guild.

An early bank in Italy, run from a stall set up in the market. Banks grew up in northern Italy in the 13th century, when merchant companies with agents in several important towns found it risky to transport money from one to another. People began to deposit money with a company in one place in return for a letter of credit, which meant that the same sum could be drawn from the company's agent in another place. Some bankers, for example the Medici of Florence, became very rich.

Africa

The Sahara, the world's largest desert, sprawls across North Africa, forming a dry, burning hot barrier between the Mediterranean lands of North Africa and the moist tropical lands to the south. But the Sahara was not a barrier to medieval traders who crossed it regularly, using the scattered oases as resting places. South of the desert lies a broad belt of savannah (tropical grassland). This region, called the Sudan, was the home of great medieval Sudanic states. South of the Sudan are the rain forests of West Africa and Zaire, where other kingdoms grew up.

On the east and south-east coasts of Africa, the Arabs found many good sites for ports. Their trade extended from East Africa as far as China. The flat coastal plains of south-central Africa are mostly narrow. Behind them, the land rises steeply to a series of high, flat plateaux. Inland travel was difficult and we know very little about this region in the Middle Ages. It was only fully explored in the 1800s.

Trade and the Sudanic States

The great Sudanic states of the Middle Ages included Ancient Ghana, Kanem-Bornu, Mali, and Songhai. Most of our knowledge about them comes from Arab writers. Some of them collected information from traders. Others travelled widely with the Arab trading caravans.

The Sudanic states gained power through trade. Arab traders brought such things as salt, textiles and tools, which they traded for gold, ivory, slaves, and hides and skins. Gold was especially important. It probably came from mines which have long ceased to exist, and was not brought up from the south where gold is mined

today. There was so much gold around that, one Arab chronicle tells us, even the royal guard dogs in Ancient Ghana had gold collars.

The peoples of the Saharan states were farmers, growing crops such as maize and groundnuts. They lived in villages, in huts built from mud baked hard in the sun. Arab reports tell us that they looked on their kings as gods. King-worship had probably spread south from Egypt down the Nile, and then westwards. Contacts with the Muslim Arabs meant that many of the Sudanic peoples were converted to Islam, and cities such as Timbuktu became great centres of Muslim learning.

CHRONOLOGY	
c325	Axum becomes Christian and conquers Kush
400	Iron-using peoples spread through south-central Africa
429–439	Vandals conquer Roman North Africa
641	Arabs conquer Egypt
683	Arabs enter Morocco
700–800	Arabs establish ports in East Africa. Ife grows up in Nigeria
800	Ancient Ghana is a major trading state in the western Sudan. Kanem-Bornu grows up to the north-east of Lake Chad
1054	Almoravid Berbers conquer Ghana
c1100	First stage of the building of Greater Zimbabwe
1250	Mali expands
1335	Songhai dynasty begins
1400s	Ife declines and Benin starts to grow. Great Bantu kingdoms grow up in south-central Africa

A caravan of camels laden with salt prepares to leave Bilma, Niger. In the Middle Ages trade in north-west Africa depended entirely on the camel, with its ability to cross the desert from one oasis to another. Two of the most important goods traded were gold, which went northwards, and salt which was taken south and which was literally worth its weight in gold. Ghana raised taxes on these goods as they passed through the kingdom, and it became immensely wealthy. Even the dogs wore collars of gold or silver.

FOREST CIVILIZATIONS

South of the savannah, in the hot, wet tropical forests, people led a very different sort of life. They cleared away patches of the forest to grow crops like cassava and plantains. From the forest itself they gathered palm nuts for food, and palm leaves for the roofs of their mud huts and for making cloth. Travel was difficult through the forests, and the kingdoms of this region were smaller than the great empires of the savannah.

As early as 250 BC, realistic terracotta sculptures were being made around the present-day village of Nok, in northern Nigeria. Many scholars believe that Nok art influenced the Yoruba sculptors of the forest kingdom of Ife. Ife, in south-west Nigeria, flourished from the 700s to the 1400s. It produced some of Africa's finest terracotta and bronze sculptures. According to tradition, an Ife master craftsmen visited Benin City, capital of the Nigerian forest kingdom of Benin, in the late 1300s. There he passed on the secrets of his art. Portuguese explorers of the 15th century were amazed by the beauty and skilled craftsmanship of the Benin bronzes.

This Benin bronze relief shows a king ('oba') and two kneeling subjects. The work of Benin craftsmen has changed very little over the centuries, and this is one reason why it is difficult to date African art with any certainty. Benin bronze-working probably began in the 15th century, with knowledge spread by Ife workers. The 'lost wax' process was used. In this, an object is modelled in wax over a clay core. Then it is covered with clay and heated until the molten wax runs out through special channels. Molten metal is poured in through these channels, and replaces exactly the form of the wax.

WHO WERE THE BUILDERS?

Great Zimbabwe is a group of massive stone ruins, including a temple and a citadel, in Zimbabwe (Rhodesia). Experts cannot agree about its origins. Some people argue that it was built by an Arab-influenced culture. Others claim that it comes from an early Black civilization.

People were living on the site as early as the 4th century AD, but the first stone buildings date only from about 1100. In the 1300s, another related people began to build larger stone buildings there and, soon afterwards, Great Zimbabwe became the centre of the Shona Karanga kingdom.

Great Zimbabwe is the only site of its kind in southern Africa. African nationalists look on it as a symbol of past glory, and so they have renamed Rhodesia, Zimbabwe. On its new flag is a design of a bird, taken from a carving on the walls of Great Zimbabwe.

Part of the ruins of the great fortified city of Zimbabwe. Stone buildings dating from this period are very rare indeed in most of Africa, and it is small wonder that the people of the region are so proud of the ancient city that they have renamed their country after it.

This Christian church, one of ten in Lalibela in Ethiopia, was carved out of solid rock. Christianity came to this region of north-east Africa when King Azana of Axum (a powerful kingdom in what is now north-east Ethiopia) was converted in the early 300s. From the 600s Axum was under pressure from Muslims to the north and east, and from pagans to the south. The Axumites finally withdrew into the mountains. There their civilization and 'Coptic' form of Christianity has survived until modern times.

Empire and Papacy

In 751 Pepin the Short overthrew the Frankish king and took the throne for himself. The pope supported him, which was very important in helping him to keep his kingdom. Twenty years later, the pope's lands in central Italy were threatened by the rulers of Lombardy to the north. He called on Pepin's son Charlemagne to help him in return. Charlemagne defeated the Lombards, and northern Italy became part of his kingdom. In 800 the pope crowned Charlemagne Roman Emperor.

All through the Middle Ages, relations between the popes and the emperors played a very important part. Sometimes they supported each other; at other times their disagreements flared into war. Sometimes a strong pope would have the final say in who would be emperor; sometimes a strong emperor would choose the pope. The countries most affected by their disputes were Germany, where the emperor was overlord of often unruly and resentful lesser rulers, and Italy which became their battleground.

Bronze water jug (13th century)

Pope Boniface II (13th century)

Below left: Otto I 'the Great' of Germany, who did much to strengthen the kingdom drawn together with difficulty by his father. In 955 he drove the Magyars from Germany and this led to a period of security and prosperity in the lands under his control. He was crowned Holy Roman emperor in 962.

GERMANY

In the north, Germany is very flat with vast plains crossed by large rivers which flow north to the sea. In the centre are rolling uplands, through which the rivers cut deep valleys. The south is much more mountainous. Even today more than a quarter of Germany is covered with forests, and in the Middle Ages trees covered much of the land.

The German king had the title 'king of the Romans' with the right to be crowned emperor by the pope at Rome. He ruled over several Germanic tribes such as the Saxons, Franconians, Swabians, and Bavarians, who had their own customs and their own dialects. The kingship was sometimes passed from father to son and was sometimes given to the strongest duke.

The emperor's great problem in Germany was to curb the power of the other great dukes. Some of them tried to do this by granting great areas of land to bishops in return for their support. For a time this worked well. But in the 11th century Churchmen felt that the emperor should not have any say in who was to be bishop. The clash came over the appointment of an archbishop for Milan in the 1070s. This was an important Church post and it was politically important too, as Milan controlled the mountain passes from Germany to north Italy. Pope Gregory VII finally excommunicated the emperor Henry IV. This was a terrible punishment which cut him off from all the rights and services of the Church. It also meant that Henry's subjects were no longer bound to be loyal to him. In order to prevent widespread revolt, Henry went to see Gregory in mid-winter at Canossa. 'And there, laying aside all the trappings of royalty, he stood in wretchedness, barefooted and clad in wool, for three days before the gate of the castle' wrote a monk at the time. Then Gregory forgave him.

At last a compromise was reached in 1122. Churchmen met in the emperor's presence to choose a bishop. He first did homage to the emperor for his lands and then he was consecrated. This particular quarrel was settled, but the struggles for land and power between the empire and the papacy broke out again many times. In the long run neither won.

In the Middle Ages Italian towns were torn by civil strife. The fighting was often between the Guelphs, who supported the papacy, and the Ghibellines, who supported the empire. In the towns, important families built towers next to their houses so that they could take refuge in them. Such towers can be seen in this picture of the town of Siena in northern Italy. From the towers people threw stones and burning pitch at their enemies in the street below. The opponents fought back with fire and heavy scaling engines.

ITALY

Much of Italy is mountainous and in the south it is very hot. The most fertile lands are in the Campagna around Naples and in the plains of Lombardy in the north. In the Middle Ages Italy had no single ruler. The lands in the centre were controlled by the popes. The south changed hands from the Byzantine empire to the Normans of Sicily, and later to the Angevins of France and the Spanish house of Aragon. Lombardy, from the time of Charlemagne on, was subject to the Roman emperor.

The balance between pope and emperor was always uneasy. When enemies such as the Muslims or Magyars threatened the Christians of Europe, the popes were quick to call for the emperors' support. But the popes did not want the emperors to become too powerful in Lombardy. There they might threaten Church lands.

In the 11th and 12th centuries a new factor emerged. The cities of Lombardy grew rich and powerful through trade. Nobles living nearby moved into the cities, and brought control of the countryside around. These cities were anxious to be independent. When emperors tried to control and tax them they joined together to fight (sometimes with the support of the pope). At other times they would fight one another for a larger share of trade. For much of the Middle Ages, northern Italy was almost constantly at war.

THE VENETIAN EMPIRE

In the Middle Ages Venice was one of the most important cities in Italy. As early as the 10th century the Venetians were trading with a large part of the Byzantine empire and Venice was becoming a wealthy city. Later, during the 12th century, there was rivalry between Venice on the east coast and Genoa on the west coast. It lasted for 200 years, but Venice was to prove the stronger. Both wanted to have control of the new trading area that had been opened up in the East. Goods from there included silk, metal-work, cloth of gold, carpets, perfumes, grain, wine, drugs and precious stones.

At this time also Venice was providing ships for the Crusaders. This proved very profitable. They were made in the arsenal (dockyard) in Venice. During the Fourth Crusade the Venetians supplied an army for the Crusaders who agreed to pay 85,000 silver marks for it. The army was made up of 4,500 horses, 4,500 knights, 9,000 squires, and 20,000 foot-soldiers. Venice also paid for the provisions of all these for a year. But, after a year, the Crusaders found that they could not pay. Instead, they decided to capture Constantinople and the Byzantine empire and share them with Venice, which they did in 1204. This helped to destroy the Eastern empire.

The Venetian empire in the late Middle Ages was made up of many trading states in the eastern Mediterranean. The area from the Aegean to Crete and Rhodes was, in fact, dominated by the Venetians. By the 14th and 15th centuries Venice was the richest commercial city in Europe.

The castle of Kyrenia in Cyprus, including the 15th-century tower built by the Venetians when Cyprus formed part of their empire.

India

The Indian subcontinent lies in South Asia, between Iran and Afghanistan on the west and Burma, Thailand, and the rest of South-East Asia on the east. To the north are the Himalayas, and beyond these mountains are Tibet and the great deserts of Chinese central Asia. The geography of India varies from high mountains, always covered in snow, to jungles and flat river plains. It was on these plains that the great cities of the Indus and the Ganges river valleys grew up.

Kingdoms of the North

A great dynasty ruled in north India from about the early 4th century AD to the end of the 5th. They were called the Guptas, and like earlier rulers they made their capital at Pataliputra in the modern state of Bihar. Their power and influence were very great, and traces of their presence are found all over north India. Cities such as Pataliputra, Rajgir, and many others were large and full of well-built houses, usually of brick. There were palaces for the rulers and the rich, Buddhist and Hindu temples, markets, and public buildings of all sorts. Houses, sometimes with several stories, were usually built around courtyards. These cities were always walled and had large gates, closed at night against intruders.

Trade and commerce flourished at this time, and the influence of Buddhist India was spread far and wide, to China and to South-East Asia.

The Guptas were eventually overthrown by the Hunds or Huns in the late 5th century. The Huns swept into India, destroying everything they found. A number of small kingdoms grew up in the wake of this confusion, ending in the 7th century with the empire of King Harsha, whose kingdom was centred at Kanarj on the Ganges. Harsha, a Buddhist, travelled far and wide in his empire seeing to its administration. This was a great age, of powerful armies, strong prosperous cities, flourishing monasteries, and busy trading.

In the later Middle Ages north India had a very complicated history, with changing dynasties and kingdoms. But these changes hardly altered the daily life of the ordinary people. Except when a fierce conqueror swept away everything of a previous rule, most people continued to live in large cities or in small villages, making a living from farming the fertile river plains.

This page of Buddhist Wisdom text, written on a palm leaf, dates from 1112. It is written in Sanskrit, a language used all over India by Buddhists and Hindus for their religious writings.

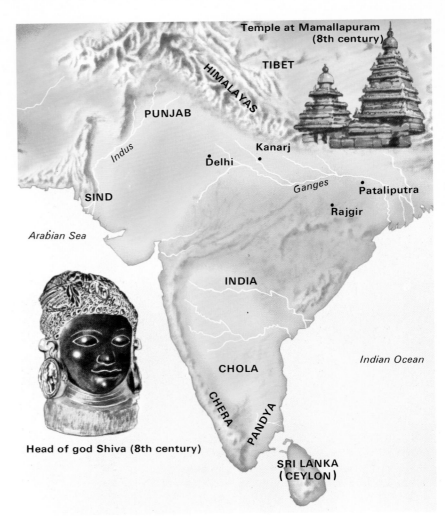

Temple at Mamallapuram (8th century)

TIBET

HIMALAYAS

PUNJAB

Indus

Delhi

Kanarj

SIND

Ganges

Pataliputra

Rajgir

Arabian Sea

INDIA

CHOLA

Indian Ocean

CHERA

PANDYA

SRI LANKA (CEYLON)

Head of god Shiva (8th century)

HINDUISM AND BUDDHISM

The two great religions of the Indian subcontinent in the Middle Ages were Hinduism and Buddhism. Hinduism dates back to well before 1000 BC, and teaches of a single world spirit, Brahman, of which all gods, people and things are a part. The Hindu law of *Dharma* teaches that everyone must obey the divine order of the universe, working to fulfil the tasks laid down for them in the position in life into which they are born. Those who succeed in this are born again into a higher position. Many gods and beliefs are accepted in the framework of Hinduism.

Buddhism was developed in the 6th century BC by the Indian Gautama. He was known as the Enlightened One, or *Buddha*. He taught that men could free themselves from the suffering of life on Earth only by obeying certain great rules. One rule, *Ahimsa*, was that no living thing should be harmed.

South India

The Tamil-speaking country in the south of of India has always had a distinctive history and style. It was made up of three kingdoms: Chola, Pandya, and Chera (Kerala). In this period the Tamils wrote a great deal of poetry, much of which was on religious subjects. Hinduism was the main religion, and many stone shrines and temples were built, some of them in caves. A large number of temple-towns were built under Chola rule, and the region was famous for its beautiful bronze figures of Hindu gods. At one time the Cholas controlled all southern India, and parts of Ceylon, Burma, Malaya and Sumatra, and traded with many other regions as well.

THE MUSLIMS IN INDIA

Muslim influence in India began in AD 711 when the Sind (now a state of modern Pakistan) was taken by the Arabs. The invasions of northern India by Mahmud of Ghazni in the the 11th century established Muslim rule as far east as the Punjab. He slew, destroyed and enslaved and, in 1022, took control of the Punjab. From that time onwards a series of Muslim dynasties established themselves in North India, doing battle with the Hindu rulers of the day.

Buddhism had died out in India after Harsha and the Muslim empires savagely persecuted the followers of the Hindu faith. Temples were looted, shrines smashed and libraries burned. The history of this part of the sub-continent up to the mid 15th century is again a series of invasions and power struggles. By the 1450s however Muslim rule was secure in north India and was to develop in the early 16th century into the great empire of the Mughals whose first ruler, Balim, came from Ferghana in central Asia.

CHRONOLOGY

455	Hephthalite Huns invade north India
600	Pallavas reach height of power in south India (to 660)
606	Harsha of Thanesar (to 647) becomes leading ruler of north of India
650	Northern India divided into many states
977	Muslims begin to raid northern India
985	Cholas reach height of power in south India and Sri Lanka (to 1044)
1022	Mahmud of Ghazni establishes Muslim rule as far east as the Punjab
1192	Northern India is under Muslim control
1196	Pala, King of north-east India, murdered by Muslims; end of Buddhism in India
1206	Sultanate of Delhi set up (to 1526)
1251	Pandyas leading dynasty in the south
1310	Muslim invaders in south
1398	Timur leads Mongol raid which devastates Delhi

Top: This huge sculpture was cut into the cliff face at Mahabalipuram, in southern India, in the 7th century AD. Mahabalipuram was the capital of the Pallava King Mammala. This carving shows a scene from the Hindu legend of Arjuna. Above: These beautiful statues of Buddha at Polonnawura in Sri Lanka (Ceylon) date from the 11th century. The written history of Sri Lanka, the great island that lies south-east of India, begins in the 6th century AD and from that time on there is a continuous record. The people of the island were converted to Buddhism in the 3rd century BC and many temples, decorated with magnificent stone sculptures, were built there. The island was often attacked by the Hindu kingdoms of south India, and for a time part of the island came under Indian rule. Tamils from southern India settled much of the north east.

The Hanseatic League

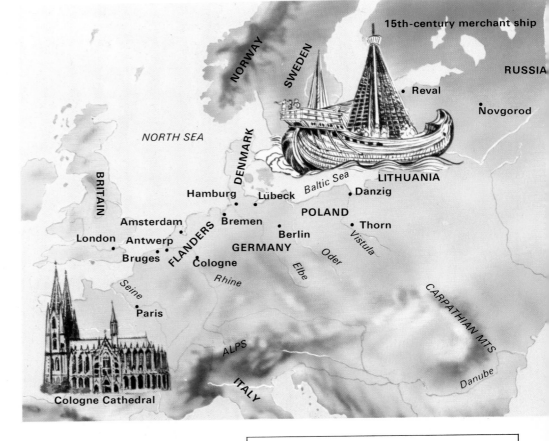

15th-century merchant ship

Cologne Cathedral

In the early Middle Ages trade in the Baltic and North Sea areas was dominated by the Vikings and Frisians. But in the late 12th and early 13th centuries, there was a change. German settlers round the Baltic gained control. Existing ports like Lübeck grew bigger, and new trading villages were founded on the Baltic coasts. Soon German merchants appeared in the Viking trading city of Novgorod in Russia. Meanwhile other German cities, among them Hamburg on the North Sea coast and Cologne on the river Rhine, were building up trade in north-west Europe.

These towns housed families of merchants who travelled far and wide. Often they were menaced by robbers and pirates. In 1241 the townspeople (burgesses) of Lübeck and Hamburg came together to make a treaty. They decided to pool their resources to safeguard the trading routes and protect each other's merchants. Soon many other towns banded together to help and protect their traders. They set up trading associations known as *hanse*, and together they are known as the Hanseatic League. Until the end of the 15th century, the League dominated the trade of northern Europe.

The Holstentor, one of the medieval gates of the north German city of Lübeck. Its position on the Baltic, between Scandinavia and the mainland of northern Europe, meant that Lübeck was an important trading centre from early on. In the 13th century it was made a free imperial city by the emperor Frederick II. It became the leading town of the Hanseatic League.

The League was at its greatest in the 14th century. No official list of member towns was drawn up, but there may have been more than a hundred. Among the most important towns were Reval, Riga, Danzig, and Thorn on the Baltic; Cologne on the Rhine; Hamburg, Bremen, Amsterdam and Antwerp on the North Sea coast. Most important of all was Lübeck. Grain, pitch, furs, timber, charcoal, flax, hemp and wax from eastern Europe were shipped from the Baltic ports. From Sweden came copper and iron. Herrings from the sea around Sweden and cod and whale oil from Norway were also important.

CHRONOLOGY

1241 Formal alliance between Lübeck and Hamburg to secure common action against robbers and pirates

1265 Towns having 'law of Lübeck' agree on common legislation to defend their merchants

1282 Lübeck and Hamburg join in 'German Hanse'

1300 All North German trading associations, towns and bases for foreign commerce are now bound together into a single league

1368 Danish War (to 1370); forces of the League defeat the Danes and safeguard their Baltic trade

1386 Union of Poland and Lithuania harms Hanseatic interests

1442 Frederick of Brandenburg gains control of Berlin

1462 Mainz loses privileges

1478 Ivan III expells Hanseatic merchants from Novgorod

1618 Thirty Years War ruins the few remaining League members (to 1648)

Privileged Settlements

The Hanse towns had trading privileges in many non-member cities, where they built settlements of warehouses and living quarters. In London their settlement was known as the Steelyard, and the merchants were given better terms for customs duties than were other traders. The Hanseatic merchants in Britain were known as Easterlings, because they came from east of the British Isles. In time the word became sterling, and was used to mean a good reliable standard of coinage.

The merchants' position in Bruges was particularly important, for here they came into contact with traders from the Mediterranean area. It was also the main market for wool from England and for Flemish cloth. In 1358 the townspeople of Bruges took away the privileges of the Hanseatic merchants. The other League towns, led by Lübeck, banned all trade with Flanders. Two years later the merchants' privileges were given back.

The League Declines

In the 15th century the Hanseatic League began to lose its strength. The main cities had been independent, but now the German states were growing more powerful. Their princes were able to overrule the merchants. In 1442 Frederick of Brandenburg gained control of the city of Berlin and the citizens had to give up their independence. Twenty years later the same thing happened in Mainz on the Rhine. Merchants were forbidden to make trading agreements with towns outside their state. In 1478 Ivan of Moscow captured Novgorod and expelled the Hanseatic merchants.

In the meantime, English and specially Dutch traders were becoming more successful. As their countries' industries grew they became less dependent on Hanseatic imports. The Dutch herring fishery increased while the catches of the Hanseatic merchants became disastrously less as changes in the climate caused fish to move their feeding grounds. With the support of the Danes, the Dutch moved into the Baltic area and became the major traders with the west.

Above: The Furriers window in the French cathedral of Chartres. Fur from Russia and the Baltic region was an important part of the Hanseatic trade.

Left: The seal of Danzig (modern Gdansk) on the Baltic Sea, a leading Hanseatic town.

Below: Novgorod in the 15th century. It was an important centre of trade in amber, furs and wax and was the farthest into Russia that the Hanse merchants reached.

MEETINGS OF MERCHANTS

The Hanseatic League had a general assembly which met at irregular intervals. It had no absolute authority, but it could bring unruly members under control. Its members met not as politicians but as businessmen to deal with problems of trade. Very occasionally they did interfere in politics, as when they forced King Waldemar of Denmark to give them control of the Sound, the channel leading from the North Sea to the Baltic. They needed this because pirates in the area often threatened fishing and merchant fleets. When it was in the Hanse's interests, their great fleets of ships could be hired out to northern rulers.

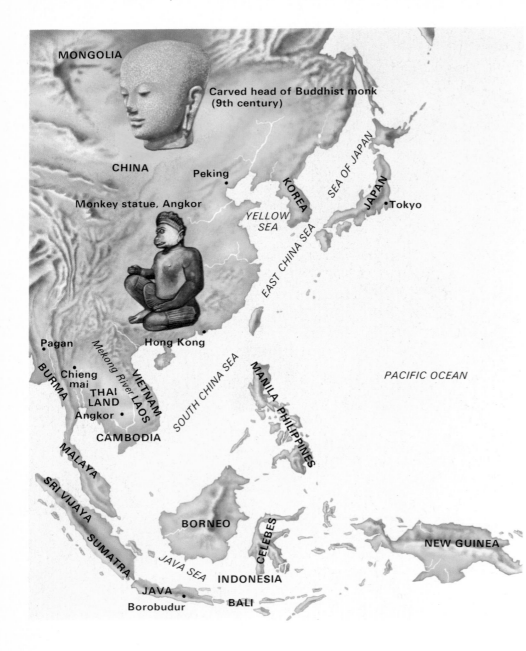

Carved head of Buddhist monk
(9th century)

Monkey statue, Angkor

MONGOLIA

CHINA

Peking

YELLOW SEA

KOREA

SEA OF JAPAN

JAPAN

•Tokyo

EAST CHINA SEA

Hong Kong

Pagan

Mekong River

BURMA

Chieng mai

THAI LAND

Angkor

CAMBODIA

VIETNAM

LAOS

SOUTH CHINA SEA

MANILA

PHILIPPINES

PACIFIC OCEAN

MALAYA

SRI VIJAYA

SUMATRA

BORNEO

CELEBES

NEW GUINEA

JAVA SEA

INDONESIA

JAVA

BALI

Borobudur

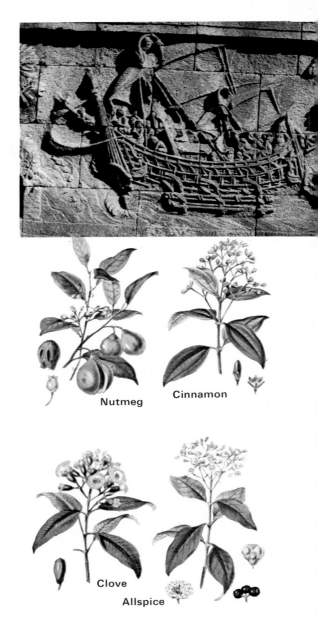

Nutmeg   Cinnamon

Clove

Allspice

South-East Asia

South-East Asia includes Burma, Thailand, Malaya, Cambodia, Laos and Vietnam, on the mainland. It also includes the great islands of modern Indonesia, Java, Bali and Sumatra, as well as Borneo, the Celebes and the Philippines. There are many rivers, mountains and steaming jungles. Most people lived in cities and villages along the great rivers. Travel by river was easier than overland. Village people were mainly fishers and farmers, and rice, then as now, was their most important crop. In the jungles lived tribal people whose lives have changed very little since ancient times.

The building of the city of Pagan started in the 11th century AD. Until the arrival of the Mongols in 1287, it was a centre of Buddhism. Many temples, like this one, still stand as a reminder of this time.

Top: A relief carving from Borobudur, dating from about 800. It shows the sort of boat which traded among the islands of South-East Asia. Above: Some of the many spices which grow in the area. They were taken to the West either by sea or by the long overland route through China, and fetched huge prices. Eventually spice traders from Europe sailed into the Indian Ocean.

Outside Influences

South-East Asia developed no common culture or common language. The two great influences there in medieval times were India and China. Traders from India settled in colonies all through South-East Asia. They brought with them the Buddhist and Hindu religions. These spread far and wide through the islands and the mainland. Chinese influence is most clearly seen in countries such as Vietnam, but evidence of trade with China is found all over the region. Chinese pottery and porcelain are excavated in nearly every part of South-East Asia, and show that trading was carried on for centuries. Chinese influence was particularly strong in technology, culture, and ways of government but not in religion.

KINGDOM OF THE KHMERS

Several very important cultures grew up in South-East Asia during the Middle Ages. Among them were those at Pagan in Burma and Chieng mai in Thailand, and the island kingdoms of Java and Bali. One of the greatest civilizations was that of the Khmers of Cambodia.

By the 5th century the Khmer people were living in a kingdom called Chenla, in the middle Mekong river region. They were Hindus, and although few of their cities have been excavated, some beautiful sculptures have been found there. In the 7th century their capital, Sambor Prei Kuk, had large public buildings and temples, built in a style rather like those in India. The Khmers had to fight off attacks by the Chams of southern Vietnam, who are often described as pirates. They caused havoc among the shipping along the coast and in the Mekong delta. The Khmers were also attacked by Indonesian kingdoms.

In the 9th century the Khmers made Angkor their capital and founded an empire that was to last for five centuries. They built a great network of irrigation canals which helped them to produce huge crops of rice from the fertile soil. Angkor has many ditches, canals, lakes and reservoirs. Early buildings at Angkor were mostly wood. These have all disappeared, leaving behind only a few statues. From the beginning of the 11th century temples were built entirely of stone. These temples are Angkor's great glory. Each king built his own, and there he carried out ceremonies to make sure of good crops. Some of the most beautiful temples were built after the Khmers were converted to Buddhism from the end of the 12th century on.

CHRONOLOGY

This relief carving of a battle scene comes from Angkor Wat, one of the great Hindu temples built at the Khmer capital of Angkor. It measures 1550 by 1420 metres (1700 by 1550 yards) and is enclosed by 6 kilometres (4 miles) of moat.

The Buddhist shrine at Borobudur in Java was built in about 800. Five square terraces rise above its square base; they are topped by three round terraces crowned by a bell-shaped 'stupa' (a building containing a relic of the Buddha or a Buddhist saint). Around it are 72 small stupas of openwork stone, each containing a figure of the Buddha.

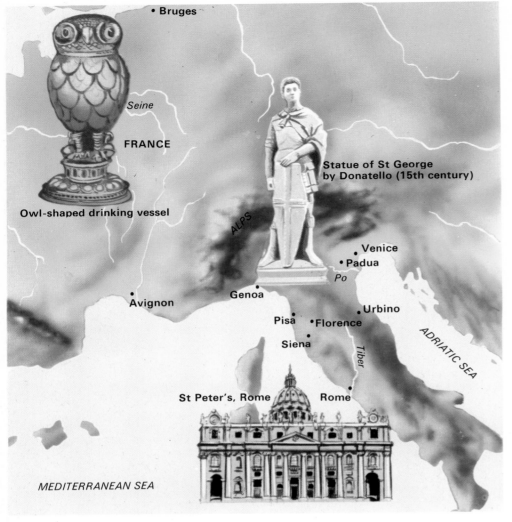

Owl-shaped drinking vessel

Statue of St George by Donatello (15th century)

St Peter's, Rome

The Renaissance

During the 13th century, the seafaring Italian cities of Venice and Genoa opened up new trade routes to the East through Constantinople. The cities of northern Italy, no longer dominated by the emperor or the pope, now found themselves at the crossroads of trade between East and West. In Florence, Genoa, Milan, Venice and elsewhere, merchants began to make huge profits from the increase in trade. Contacts with the East gave them a wider outlook and a new interest in collecting rare and exotic things. Wealth and fashion led to astonishing advances in learning and the arts.

This period in Western civilization is called the Renaissance, a word meaning 'rebirth'. A new, adventurous spirit began to disturb the settled world of the Middle Ages, making way for an age of exploration, discovery, and scientific thought.

The poet Dante (1265–1321); behind him is his native city of Florence. He wrote in his native language, a north Italian speech called Tuscan. Before his time, Italians had preferred to write in French or Latin.

Trade and Travel

Italian merchants travelled far and wide. In the 1270s the Venetian Marco Polo took the route through Central Asia to China, then ruled by the Mongol emperor Kublai Khan. Italians traded in London and Flanders (Belgium), and along the shores of the Black Sea. They brought raw materials such as wool, hides and precious metals back to Italy. There, skilled craftsmen turned them into finished goods, which were exported at a profit.

A system of banking grew up to support trade. A banker would lend a merchant the money to cover the period between buying, say, wool in northern Europe and selling it in Florence. The famous banks of Florence came to lend money to kings. One banking and trading family, the Medicis, came to rule Florence itself for more than 200 years. All over northern Italy, powerful families and groups of merchants beautified their cities with splendid new buildings. In Rome, too, several popes were patrons of artists and scholars.

The New Learning

In the late Middle Ages trade made northern Italy the wealthiest region in Europe. Italian merchant-princes competed to make their native cities brilliant centres of learning and the arts. There was a great fashion for collecting libraries. Agents were sent all over Europe to bring back rare manuscripts by famous Greek and Roman authors of the ancient world. Many were found in monastery libraries where they had long been forgotten. As few people could understand the ancient Greek and Latin in which they were written, scholars translated them into Italian. More and more people rediscovered the ideas and discoveries of Greek and Roman civilization, which the Church had long condemned as 'pagan'.

This painting by Piero della Francesca (c. 1415–1492) is of the Duke of Urbino, Federigo da Montefeltro. A mercenary general, he spent much of his money on building churches, hospitals, and schools for his people and in caring for the poor. At his beautiful palace he collected a famous library.

The Arts

The Renaissance saw great changes in the arts. At the beginning of the period, most architects and painters were simply craftsmen. They were expected to work to old-established styles and patterns. In architecture the style was Gothic, in which windows and arches were pointed, and the roofs were decorated with tall pinnacles. But in the 1420s the Florentine architect Brunelleschi began to build in the style he had learned from ancient Roman buildings. They were carefully balanced, with rounded arches and domes.

In painting the medieval style was originally influenced by Byzantine art. Figures were flat and stylized against plain gold backgrounds. But around 1300 a painter called Giotto began to paint figures more realistically, making them appear more solid and setting them against backgrounds that looked like the real world. As time went on artists and architects developed these advances even farther.

By the end of the Renaissance, artists, sculptors and architects were known far and wide by name. Men like Leonardo da Vinci, Michelangelo and Raphael travelled from city to city where they were received as honoured guests by powerful men.

THE RENAISSANCE AND THE CHURCH

Italy's great reputation as a centre of science and the arts drew scientists, scholars and painters from all over Europe. During the 15th century the development of the printing press in Germany helped to spread the latest advances in learning. One result of this was that people began to question the traditional teachings of the Church, which had come to seem narrow and old-fashioned. The Dutch scholar Erasmus studied in Italy before returning to northern Europe. In his writings he criticized Church attitudes, and produced an edition of the New Testament based on the original Greek text, instead of the Latin text used by the Church. Such activities directly challenged the Church's authority, and encouraged people to read the scriptures for themselves, rather than simply accept what the Church told them. This new questioning and criticism finally caused the Church to split into two factions, Catholic and Protestant. The united western Church of the Middle Ages had gone for ever.

A bronze panel by the sculptor Lorenzo Ghiberti of Florence (1378–1455). It is in the style of ancient sculpture, with natural looking figures, unlike the stiffer and more formal sculpture of the Middle Ages. It shows Abraham about to sacrifice Isaac.

CHRONOLOGY
1250 Italy split into many separate city states. Those in north and central Italy gain wealth and power. Southern Italy remains poor
1275 Marco Polo reaches Peking
1305 Papal See removed from Rome to Avignon
1306 Giotto completes series of frescoes in Padua
1307 Dante begins to write 'Divine Comedy'
1341 Petrarch crowned Poet Laureate
1348 Black Death ravages Europe
1353 Boccaccio finishes writing the 'Decameron'
1397 Medici bank founded in Florence
1402 Ghiberti wins competition for Baptistry doors, Florence
1434 Cosimo de'Medici rules Florence
1447 Pope Nicholas V founds the Vatican Library
1463 Venice begins 16-year war with Ottoman Turks
1465 First printing press in Italy

Florence was one of the richest cities in northern Italy and its wealthy merchants lived in great luxury. Some citizens disapproved very much of their way of life. In 1494 the friar Savonarola was made ruler of Florence. He built great bonfires on which precious possessions were burned (below) and preached many sermons telling people to give up their sinful way of life. Eventually Savonarola made many powerful enemies, and he was sentenced to death in 1498.

Before Columbus

Perhaps the first European to reach the Americas was the Irish monk St Brendan in the 6th century AD, who sailed west from Ireland in a boat made of leather. Early in the 11th century, Vikings from Greenland reached the coast of North America (see page 25). They never managed to set up successful colonies there, and the native people were unfriendly. Their last visits were early in the 14th century.

It was almost 200 years before the next Europeans reached the Americas. This time they were Spaniards, who landed first in Central America in 1519 and then in South America. There they found great civilizations which had grown up quite independently of the civilizations in the rest of the world. The most important were the empires of the Aztecs in Mexico and the Incas of Peru. Within a few years, the Spaniards had almost totally destroyed them as they conquered and converted the local peoples.

The lands ruled by both the Aztecs and the Incas were mountainous but fertile. It was possible to grow good crops there, especially after people learned how to bring water to the fields through systems of irrigation channels. Maize was a very important crop, and beans, squashes, hot chili peppers, and avocados were grown. In the high Andes, where it was too cold for maize, potatoes were the most important food. The gold disc below was made by the Chimu people of north Peru in the 12th or 13th century AD. In the centre is the Earth Goddess. The various sections of the disc are a calendar for sowing the main crops.

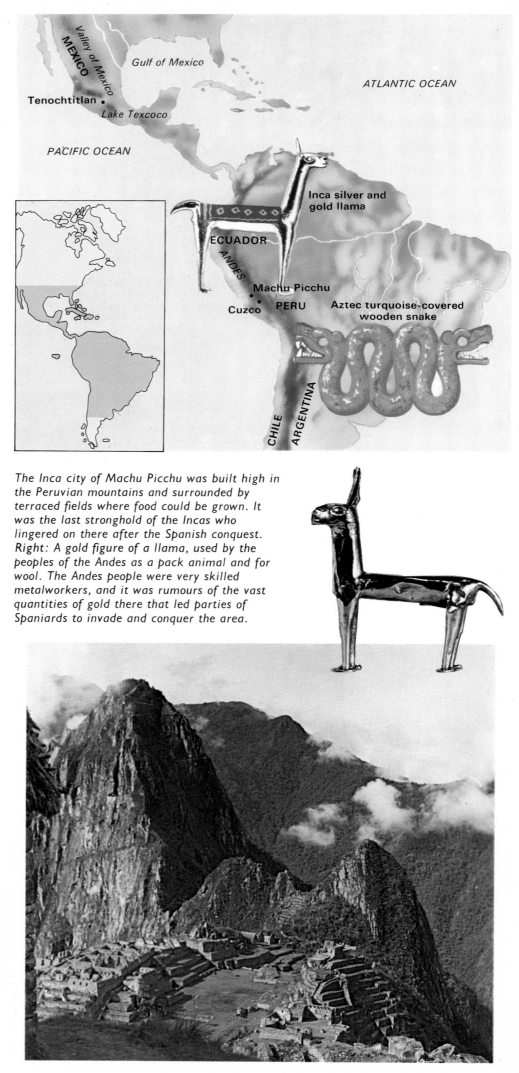

The Inca city of Machu Picchu was built high in the Peruvian mountains and surrounded by terraced fields where food could be grown. It was the last stronghold of the Incas who lingered on there after the Spanish conquest. Right: A gold figure of a llama, used by the peoples of the Andes as a pack animal and for wool. The Andes people were very skilled metalworkers, and it was rumours of the vast quantities of gold there that led parties of Spaniards to invade and conquer the area.

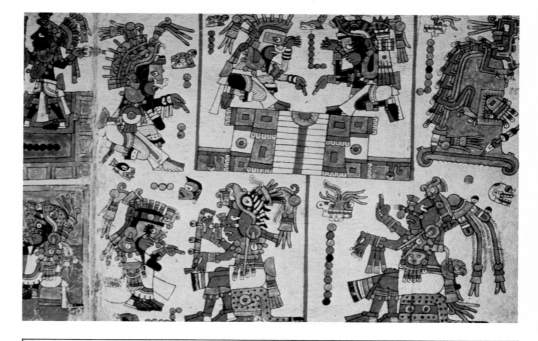

The Incas

In the 15th century the Incas built up a vast empire in South America. It stretched from modern Quito in Ecuador south through Peru into Chile and Argentina. Much of it was in the Andes mountains, where there are grazing lands and fertile valleys between the high peaks. Along the coasts are flat deserts where only the land around the rivers can be farmed.

The ruling Incas came from a family which settled in the highland village of Cuzco in the 12th century. In the mid-15th century they conquered the highland area and then the Chimú empire along the coast. The Incas controlled 6 million people by strict and ruthless government. All land belonged to the state, and everyone had to spend much of their time working for the emperor. Armies and messengers could travel swiftly through the empire along a network of roads.

The peoples of the Inca empire were skilled craftsmen. They made beautifully decorated pots, and gold and silver ornaments and jewellery. Their weavers made brightly patterned cloth, sometimes working feathers into it. The Incas were also great builders, and ruins of their vast stone cities and temples still stand high in the mountains.

CHRONOLOGY

500	Tiahuanaco-Huari expansion in the Andes; Mochica and Nazca cultures in coastal Peru; Maya Classic Period in Central America (to 900); Teotihuacan important in Mexico
980	Toltecs establish their capital at Tula in Mexico
1000	Huari empire breaks up
1151	Toltec empire falls
1325	Aztecs found Tenochtitlan
1370	Chimu kingdom grows in coastal Peru
1428	Aztecs win independence
1438	Inca empire is built up in Peru and neighbouring countries
1440	Aztecs begin to build up their empire
1450	Incas conquer Chimu kingdom
1521	Hernan Cortes conquers Tenochtitlan
1533	Francisco Pizarro conquers Incas

THE AZTECS

When the Spaniards arrived in Mexico in 1519 the Aztec empire stretched from the Atlantic Ocean to the Pacific Ocean. The Aztecs ruled it from their capital of Tenochtitlan, built on a swampy island in the middle of Lake Texcoco. It housed over half a million people.

The Aztecs had arrived in the Valley of Mexico at the end of the 12th century. At first they were slaves but before long they became independent. They built up their empire during the 15th century, forcing the tribes around them to pay a heavy tribute. This included food such as maize and beans, luxuries, and raw materials for craftsmen in gold, silver, and jade to work with. Traders brought turquoises from the Pueblo Indians to the north, and from the south came brightly coloured parrot feathers which were made into capes, fans, and head-dresses.

The Aztecs were ruled by their emperor. Next in importance were officials including judges, army commanders, and the governors of conquered provinces. They were given their own land and were allowed to wear ornaments of gold and precious stones. Then came free commoners, grouped into clans, and below them landless peasants and slaves. Every Aztec boy served in the army from 17 to 22. Some stayed on, for a peasant could rise to be a commander.

The priests were a special class. There were several thousand of them in Tenochtitlan alone. The Aztec religion was very cruel, and prisoners of war were sacrificed to gods such as the war god Huitzilopochtli and the rain god Tlaloc.

The Turks

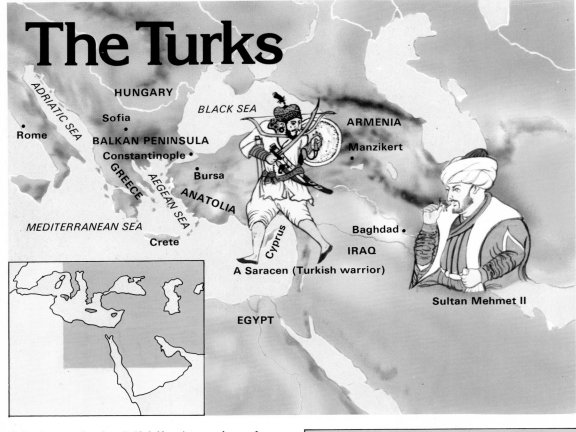

HUNGARY
BLACK SEA
Sofia
Rome
BALKAN PENINSULA
Constantinople •
ARMENIA
Manzikert •
Bursa •
ANATOLIA
MEDITERRANEAN SEA
Crete
Cyprus
Baghdad •
IRAQ
EGYPT
A Saracen (Turkish warrior)
Sultan Mehmet II
ADRIATIC SEA
GREECE
AEGEAN SEA

Above: A decorative panel from the Seljuk period.

Below: Bursa was the capital of the early Ottoman sultans before the fall of Constantinople in 1453. Today the ruined walls of the citadel mark the site of the old fortified city. By the road leading west from the town is the Muradiye Mosque. It was built by Murad II in the 15th century. Many other tombs and monuments have been built around it and in the cemetery shown here are buried 11 Ottoman princes and princesses. Elsewhere in Bursa are the tombs of Osman and Orhan, founders of the Ottoman dynasty.

All through the Middle Ages, invaders from Central Asia menaced the civilized areas of the world. In many cases, these nomads settled down in the countries they conquered and adopted at least some of their ways. This is what happened to the Turks, a nomadic people who came to the Near East as invaders and who ended up in control of the great Islamic empire.

CHRONOLOGY	
970	Seljuk Turks become Muslim
1055	Seljuks seize Baghdad
1064	Seljuks take Armenian capital and raid Byzantine territory
1071	Seljuks defeat Byzantines at Manzikert
1288	Osman becomes leader of 'Ottoman' Turks, who from now on gain land from empire
1326	Bursa becomes Ottoman capital
1385	Sofia falls to Ottomans
1389	Ottomans defeat Serbs
1402	Ottomans temporarily defeated by Mongols
1453	Ottomans under Mehmet capture Constantinople

The Seljuks

The Turks were warlike nomads whose homeland was east-central Asia. They are first heard of under the Chinese name of T'u Kue in the 6th century AD. In the 10th century Muslim missionaries converted many of them to Islam, and soon afterwards a large group of Turks moved westwards under their leader Seljuk. They came right into the heart of the Islamic empire, and in 1055 they reached Baghdad.

At this time the caliph of Baghdad was the ruler of all Islam. Under him were sultans who ruled over different regions. The caliph hoped that the Seljuks would support him. They used the title of sultan, and soon became excellent administrators of Islamic lands and ways of life. They gained control of much of the Near East.

Next the Seljuks moved northwards to the Byzantine empire. They defeated a large Byzantine army and moved into Anatolia, where they established a large sultanate. Although fighting broke out many times, they managed to build up a prosperous state. Agriculture and mining production improved, and trade with Europe increased with the help of Italian merchants.

The Ottomans

In the mid-13th century Mongols from Central Asia devastated Anatolia and the Near East. After a time of great confusion, a new powerful state grew up in Anatolia. It was ruled by the Ottoman Turks, whose first great leader was called Osman. The Ottomans gained control of the Balkan Peninsula from the Byzantines. Many people there had suffered under Byzantine rule, and welcomed the Ottomans. With the help of soldiers from the Balkan countries the Ottomans soon controlled almost all of Anatolia. Constantinople and the land around it remained a tiny outpost of Christianity in this Muslim empire. Another wave of Mongol raiders halted the Ottomans only briefly. In 1453 they captured Constantinople. The great Byzantine church of Holy Wisdom (Hagia Sophia) was proclaimed a mosque, but much of the city was left alone. As in the other Ottoman lands, many people remained Christian.

Soon the Ottomans ruled over an enormous empire which stretched from Algeria along the south Mediterranean coast, south to the Sudan, and east into Iraq. They kept control of the Balkans and pushed northwards far into Hungary. The Ottomans were able to rule such an enormous area because they were efficient governors. They had a network of central and local officials which spread down into tiny villages. Trade with Europe and the East brought wealth. Above all, the Muslim way of life, with religion giving guidance on every aspect of daily living, helped to keep the Ottoman empire together.

By 1453 the Turks had conquered all the Byzantine territory except the capital Constantinople. The Turkish leader Sultan Mehmet II (right) was determined to capture Constantinople. For more than a year he made plans and then his troops laid siege to the city (below). It was six weeks before Constantinople fell. This painting shows the Turks camped outside the city. They are bombarding the walls with cannon. The Ottoman empire now became the greatest of all the Muslim states. Ottoman domination, under the sultan, lasted until the 20th century.

THE JANISSARIES

The Ottoman sultan needed many soldiers to protect and control his empire. The most famous of his troops were the *Janissaries*. They were first recruited in the late 14th century and their name comes from the Turkish words for 'new forces'. The early Janissaries were battle captives. Later they came from the many slaves who were collected from Christian villages in the empire as children, and then converted to Islam.

The Janissaries were very fierce and brave and in the 15th and 16th centuries they were thought to be unbeatable. In peace time they staffed frontier towns and policed Istanbul (Constantinople). When the Janissaries were unhappy with their conditions they kicked over the great copper cauldrons in which their food was cooked. Everyone dreaded this, for the Janissaries were very powerful and even helped to overthrow several sultans.

The World in 1450

This is an age of change in Europe. The feudal system is dying out, accelerated by the devastation of the Black Death. The invention of gunpowder has changed the old ways of battle and defence. Independent trading cities in northern Italy see a new interest in art and learning which spreads through Europe. Scholarship and scientific knowledge grow and spread, helped by the invention of the printing press in the 1450s. Soon the western Church will be split by the break away of the Protestants in the Reformation. In 1453 the last remnant of the Byzantine empire falls to the Ottoman Turks whose rule will last to the 20th century. The great age of exploration is about to begin.

15th-century gold pin, found in the British Isl

The Americas Two great empires have now grown up: the Aztec empire of Mexico and the Inca empire of Peru. Both will be overthrown by the Spanish *conquistadors* in the next century.

3 Western Europe After the Black Death in the mid-14th century the feudal system has broken down and been replaced by central government. England and France struggle in the Hundred Years War; when it ends in 1453 almost all England's French possessions are lost. In Italy, the wealthy northern towns take an increasing interest in learning and in the arts, in a movement which we know as the Renaissance. This soon spreads north. The Muslims are finally driven from Spain in 1492. In Germany Gutenberg invents his printing process.

Above: A 15th-century tournament shield. Below: Agincourt (1415), a great English victory over the French.

Inca gold figure, Peru

The Portuguese Prince Henry the Navigator (1394–1460) took a great interest in exploration. He sent sailors farther down the west coast of Africa than they had ever gone before. At Sagres on the Atlantic coast of Portugal he brought together the finest map-makers, mathematicians, astronomers, pilots, and designers of ships. His work and encouragement led to the great explorations which took place soon after his death.

9 Far East Under the Ming dynasty trade and scholarship revive in China. Colonists spread
10 Chinese ways to Malaya and the East Indies.

Statue of a horseman, Italy

Icon of Christ, northern Russia

Ottoman plate, Turkey

Porcelain vase, China

The technique of enamelling metal spread from Italy to Hungary in the early 15th century and Hungarian work became famous. This superb chalice was made at the beginning of the 16th century.

5 India Muslim Mongols gain control of northern India and in 1526 set up the Mughal empire there. In the south Hindu kingdoms remain in power. On the west coast Arabs dominate trade.

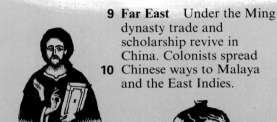

Benin altar head, West Africa

6 The Byzantine Empire In 1453 the Ottoman Turks capture Constantinople and the empire finally disappears.

7 Eastern Europe Much of Russia is now under Tartar control. In the north, Moscow grows increasingly strong after 1462 under Ivan the Great. Trade in the Baltic is now increasingly in Flemish
8 hands. Poland is growing into a large and powerful state; Hungary is soon threatened by the Turks. In Bohemia John Hus's teachings have threatened a break from the Roman Church.

4 Africa The Benin kingdom rises in the western forest region. Soon the first Portuguese explorers and traders will reach the coastal areas.

11 Islam The Ottoman Turks capture Constantinople in 1453 and build up an empire including North Africa, Egypt, Arabia, Anatolia (now known as Turkey) and south-east Europe.

Index

Glossary

Architect Planner and designer of buildings.
Barbarian One living beyond the frontiers of a dominant country.
Bishopric Office of bishop and all the area controlled by him.
Bubonic Plague (Black Death) Disease spread to Europe from Asia by rats carried on trading ships. Its name comes from the blackening of the skin caused by internal bleeding.
Caravan Group of merchants or pilgrims travelling together, usually for safety.
Chronicle Account of the events of a period of time set down in the order in which they happened.
Colonize Found settlements abroad.
Crop rotation Method of farming in which a field is planted with a different crop each year for two or three years, and each crop replaces the goodness taken from the soil by the last.

Merchant One who makes a living through trade, especially wholesale trade with foreign countries.
Migration The movement of a body of people from one area to another.
Moors Name given to a race of Muslims living in North Africa, who in the 8th century conquered Spain.
Mosaic Art form in which tiny pieces of glass or stone of different colours are joined together to produce a picture.
Nomads People who move from summer grazing lands to winter grazing lands with their flocks and herds.
Patron One who gives money and support to a person with talent but no money or influence.
Peddlar One who makes his living by travelling around selling small items.
Relic Part of the body or belongings of a holy person, kept after his death as a religious object.
Saga A story of heroic deeds told and passed on by word of mouth.
Shrine Holy place, usually on a site where some important event connected with a religion took place, or where relics are kept.
Stupa A Buddhist monument containing a relic.
Steppes High cold plains of Russia and Central Asia.
Technology Practical use of scientific ideas.
Terracotta Shaped and baked clay, usually brownish red in colour, often painted and glazed for decoration.
Tribute Payment of money or goods made by one person or state to another of higher authority, in acknowledgement of submission or in return for peace and protection.

Culture Skills and way of life of a people or society.
Dynasty Series of rulers from the same family.
Excavation The unearthing of an historic site.
Excommunication Punishment issued by the Pope which removed the right to the forgiveness of sins or a Christian burial. If a ruler was excommunicated, his subjects were often excommunicated as well.
Feudalism System whereby a ruler or great lord owns the land and grants it to lesser lords or peasants in return for service.
Flood plain The area around a river which is affected when the river floods. The soil is usually very fertile as a result of the silt which is laid down.
Freemason A stonemason who has perfected his craft and who is therefore allowed to carve the decorative stonework on important buildings.
Glazier One whose trade is to construct the windows of buildings, in particular the stained glass windows of churches.
Great Wall Huge defence system, some 2400 kilometres (1500 miles) long built by the Chinese during the Chin dynasty. It was built of earth and stone, and much of it remains today.
Horde A large tribe or troop of nomadic warriors.
Hanse German word for a company of merchants.
Irrigate To supply fields with water.
Manuscript Hand-written document or book.
Medieval Word used to describe something which is connected with the Middle Ages.

ACKNOWLEDGEMENTS

Photographs: Front cover Picturepoint; endpapers Sonia Halliday, title page Ronald Sheridan; page 6 Alan Hutchison (top), Trinity College, Dublin (centre right), British Museum (below right); 6–7 Giraudon; 7 Scala/Cividale, Museo Archeologico; 8 Salisbury Cathedral/Michael Holford (top), Bibliothèque Nationale, Paris (below); 9 Sonia Halliday (top), Michael Holford (bottom left), British Museum (bottom right); 11 Scala/Cividale, Museo Archeologico; 12 Victoria and Albert Museum (top), Giraudon (bottom), Mansell Collection (right); 13 BBC Hulton Picture Library (top left), Bodleian Library (top right), Scala/Firenze, Museo dell'Opera del Duomo (below); 14 British Museum (top), Sonia Halliday (bottom); 15 Sonia Halliday (top), Scala/Firenze, Bargello (bottom); 16 Georgina Herrmann (right), Sonia Halliday (bottom left); 17 Middle East Archives (top right), British Museum (centre left) British Museum (bottom); 18 Sonia Halliday (left), Michael Holford (right); 19 Bildarchiv Österreichische Nationalbibliothek (top left), Giraudon (top right), Sonia Halliday (bottom left); 20 Victoria and Albert Museum (top right), British Museum (left); 21 Alan Hutchison (top), Bibliothèque Nationale, Paris (bottom); 23 Michael Holford (top); 24 ZEFA; 25 Universitets Oldsaksamling, Oslo (top), Werner Foreman Archive (bottom); 27 Giraudon; 29 Louvre, Paris (bottom); 30–31 Courtesy of the Smithsonian Institution, Freer Gallery of Art, Washington DC; 31 Seattle Art Museum (top), ZEFA (bottom); 32 Michael Holford (centre), Mary Evans Picture Library; 33 British Museum (centre), Mary Evans Picture Library; 34 David Williamson; 35 ZEFA (top right), Interfoto MTI, Budapest (bottom left); 36 Alan Hutchison (top left), Topkapi Museum, Istanbul (right); 37 Edinburgh University; 39 British Museum (top), ZEFA (bottom); 40 Giraudon, Paris; 41 Sonia Halliday/Bibliothèque Nationale, Paris; 42 Sonia Halliday; 43 Peter Clayton (top right), Sonia Halliday (bottom left), C R Warn (bottom right); 44 Scala/Aquisgrana, Duomo (top); 45 Scala/Siena, Pinacoteca Nazionale (top), Sonia Halliday (bottom); 46 Michael Holford; 47 ZEFA (top), Alan Hutchison (bottom); 48 ZEFA; 49 Sonia Halliday (top right), Bildarchiv Preussischer Kulturbesitz (left), Mansell Collection (bottom right); 50 Mansell Collection (bottom right); 51 Robert Harding; 52 Scala/Firenze, Museo dell'Opera del Duomo (right); 53 Giraudon (top left), Scala/Firenze, Baptistery (right); 54 Michael Holford (top left), J. Allan Cash (bottom right); 55 British Museum; 56 Turkish Tourist Office (top right), Sonia Halliday (bottom right); 57 Sonia Halliday (top), Sonia Halliday/Bibliothèque Nationale, Paris (bottom); 58 British Museum; 59 ZEFA.
Picture Research: Elizabeth Rudoff.